The Véroniqu
French Langua

THE ULTIMATE FRENCH VOCABULARY QUIZ BOOK FOR BEGINNER & INTERMEDIATE LEVELS

550 Practice Questions

BONUSES: French Idioms & French Literary Quotes

By Véronique F. Courtois, MA, MS
The Sorbonne-Nouvelle, Paris III, France
Former Instructor, Tufts University &
Boston University, Massachusetts
The French Library in Boston, Massachusetts,
The Beverly Hills Lingual Institute, Beverly Hills, California,
The French Alliance of Los Angeles, California

ISBN 9780998080475

Dear Student of French,

This quiz book is the study companion to THE ULTIMATE FRENCH GRAMMAR QUIZ BOOK for Beginner and Intermediate levels. It is intended for you if you are:

A Francophile who studied French years ago and needs to refresh his/her French vocabulary skills.

A high school or a university student taking a French class and seeking a quick general review before an exam.

These quiz questions are intended to help you assess the vocabulary you need to master to pass your French tests or exams.

Vocabulary lists categorized per theme are not included in this Quiz Book as they are widely available for free or for purchase online.

The more you practice these questions and review the corresponding material, the better prepared you will be when sitting for your exams.

You can contact me through my Facebook Page:
www.facebook.com/VeroniqueFCourtoisBooks

Or my email address: **vfcfrenchtutoring@gmail.com**

Merci et bonne chance !
Véronique

LISTE DES CHAPITRES

CHAPITRE 1

Présentation & salutations / Introduction & Greetings

I/ Choisissez la bonne réponse :

1/ Mon _____ est Sonia et mon _____ est Smith.
    a/ nom de famille/prénom
    b/ prénom/diminutif
    c/ prénom/nom de famille
    d/ diminutif/surnom

2/ Je/J'_____ vingt-cinq ans et je/j'_____ en France.
    a/ suis/habite
    b/ ai/réside
    c/ as/habite
    d/ ai/vit

3/ Êtes-vous marié ? Non, je suis _____.
    a/ mort
    b/ exténué
    c/ en avance
    d/ célibataire

4/ Quel plaisir ! Je suis _____ de vous rencontrer !
    a/ dégouté
    b/ fatigué
    c/ déprimé
    d/ enchanté

5/ J'espère te revoir très _____.
    a/ prochainement
    b/ prudemment
    c/ lentement
    d/ doucement

II/ *Éliminez l'intrus :*

1/ bonjour/salut/coucou/bienvenue/adieu

2/ à plus tard/tout de suite/à mercredi/à bientôt/à demain

3/ une nationalité/un pays/un citoyen/des études/un passeport

4/ un prénom/un nom/un diminutif/une naissance/un surnom

5/ ravi/déçu/enchanté/plaisir/joyeux

III/ *Complétez les phrases avec les mots proposés :*

a/ un métier	b/ une veuve	c/ à tout à l'heure
d/ Quoi de neuf ?		e/ une nièce

1/ ___ : une activité professionnelle.

2/ ___ : expression utilisée pour demander des nouvelles.

3/ ___ : une femme qui perdu son mari.

4/ ___ : la fille d'un frère ou d'une sœur.

5/ ___ : synonyme de « à plus tard »

IV/ *Écrivez le nom qui correspond au verbe ou le verbe qui correspond au nom :*

1/ habiter : _____.

2/ une naissance : _____.

3/ se présenter : _____.

4/ un plaisir : _____.

5/ espérer : _____.

6/ un mariage : _____.

7/ employer : _____.

8/ accueillir : _____.

9/ décevoir : _____.

10/ un divorce : _____.

V/ Traduisez les phrases suivantes :

1/ What foreign language do you speak?

_____.

2/ How are you?

_____.

3/ What country were you born in?

_____.

4/ Do you have brothers and sisters?

_____.

5/ What is your job/profession?

_____.

Réponses / Answer Key / Chapitre 1

I	II	III
1/ c	1/ adieu	1/ a
2/ b	2/ tout de suite	2/ d
3/ d	3/ des études	3/ b
4/ d	4/ une naissance	4/ e
5/ a	5/ déçu	5/ c

IV	
1/ une habitation	6/ se marier
2/ naître	7/ un emploi
3/ une présentation	8/ un accueil
4/ plaire	9/ une déception
5/ un espoir	10/ divorcer

V
1/ Quelle langue étrangère parlez-vous ?
2/ Comment allez-vous ?
3/ Dans quel pays êtes-vous né(e) ?
4/ Avez-vous/As-tu des frères et (des) sœurs ?
5/ Quel est votre métier/profession ?

CHAPITRE 2

Les jours, les mois, l'heure / Days, Months, Telling time

I/ *Choisissez la bonne réponse :*

1/ Il y a quatre_____ et douze _____ dans l'année.
   a/ mois/saisons
   b/ saisons/mois
   c/ saison/semaine
   d/ saisons/moi

2/ Lundi, _____, mercredi, ____, vendredi, ____, dimanche.
   a/ mardi, samedi, jeudi
   b/ jeudi, mardi, samedi
   c/ samedi, jeudi, mardi
   d/ mardi, jeudi, samedi

3/ Il doit être _____ parce que j'ai faim.
   a/ minuit
   b/ minute
   c/ le midi
   d/ midi

4/ Le deuxième et le septième mois de l'année sont :
   a/ janvier/juillet
   b/ février/juillet
   c/ février/août
   d/ février/juin

5/ Nous prenons nos vacances d'été en _____ .
   a/ mars/août
   b/ juillet/janvier
   c/ avril/juin
   d/ juillet/août

II/ Éliminez l'intrus :

1/ un été/un matin/une journée/un soir/une nuit

2/ septembre/octobre/l'hiver/novembre/décembre

3/ lundi/jeudi/une matinée/samedi/mercredi

4/ une minute/une seconde/une heure/une demi-heure/dimanche

5/ une décennie/hier/un mois/une année/un siècle

III/ Masculin ou féminin :

1/ après-midi : _____	6/ minute : _____
2/ soir : _____	7/ saison : _____
3/ printemps : _____	8/ quart d'heure : _____
4/ heure : _____	9/ hiver : _____
5/ semaine : _____	10/ trimestre : _____

IV/ Écrivez les heures suivantes en toutes lettres :

1/ 15h40 : _____

2/ 6h15 : _____

3/ 20h05 : _____

4/ 12h00 : _____

5/ 8h35 : _____

V/ Associez les activités suivantes à la saison la plus pertinente (printemps, été, automne, hiver) :

1/ Les abricots sont prêts à être cueillis : _____.

2/ On fait du ski nordique en montagne : _____.

3/ Les feuilles des arbres changent de couleur : _____.

4/ Les oiseaux font leur nid : _____.

5/ Les enfants adorent aller à la plage : _____.

BONUS : *Quelques expressions idiomatiques :*

1/ À tout à l'heure : dans quelques instants

2/ À la bonne heure : tant mieux ! Voilà qui est bien !

3/ De bonne heure : tôt le matin

4/ Passer un mauvais/sale quart d'heure : vivre un moment difficile

BONUS : *Deux dictions populaires :*

1/ En avril, ne te découvre pas d'un fil : il fait encore frais au mois d'avril alors il vaut mieux continuer à s'habiller chaudement.

2/ En mai, fais ce qu'il te plaît : au mois de mai, vous pouvez faire ce que vous désirez.

Réponses / Answer Key :

I	II	III	
1/ b	1/ un été	1/ M ou F	6/ F
2/ d	2/ l'hiver	2/ M	7/ F
3/ d	3/ une matinée	3/ M	8/ M
4/ b	4/ dimanche	4/ F	9/ M
5/ d	5/ hier	5/ F	10/ M

IV
1/ Quinze heures quarante ou quatre heures moins vingt
2/ Six heures quinze ou six heures et quart
3/ Vingt heures cinq ou huit heures cinq
4/ midi ou minuit
5/ huit heures trente-cinq ou neuf heures moins vingt-cinq

V		
1/ en été	2/ en hiver	3/ en automne
4/ au printemps	5/ en été	

CHAPITRE 3

La description physique / Physical Characteristics

I/ Choisissez la bonne réponse :

1/ Quand vous êtes roux, vous avez souvent les _____.
    a/ yeux bleus/la peau blanche
    b/ yeux marron/la peau blanche
    c/ yeux bleus/la peau mate
    d/ yeux noirs/la peau blanche

2/ Un homme qui a perdu ses cheveux est _____
    a/ chauvin
    b/ chauve
    c/ chauve-souris
    d/ chaud

3/ _____ sont des organes vitaux.
    a/ L'orteil/le cœur/les poumons
    b/ Le cœur/l'oreille/le cerveau
    c/ Le foie/le cœur/les reins
    d/ Le bras/le cerveau/le pancréas

4/ Un homme qui a du poil au menton est _____
    a/ barbant
    b/ barbu
    c/ barde
    d/ barda

5/ Je ne porte pas de lunettes mais des _____ de contact.
    a/ rousquilles
    b/ pastilles
    c/ lenteurs
    d/ lentilles

II/ *Choisir les adjectifs appropriés pour décrire les personnes suivantes :*

pâle, roux, costaud, souple, grassouillet, bronzée, élancée, frisé, rond

1/ Sara fait du volley-ball au soleil : elle est _____

2/ Marie fait beaucoup de yoga : elle est _____

3/ Kevin est déménageur : il est _____

4/ Chloé est mannequin : elle est _____

5/ Cyril mange trop de gâteaux : il est _____

III/ *Trouver les noms qui correspondent aux verbes suivants :*

1/ se raser : _____

2/ voir : _____

3/ boire : _____

4/ croître : _____

5/ vieillir : _____

IV/ *Trouvez le contraire des adjectifs suivants :*

1/ des épaules larges : _____

2/ un beau visage : _____

3/ des oreilles rondes : _____

4/ un corps sain : _____

5/ des yeux éteints : _____

V/ *Traduisez les phrases suivantes :*

1/ Her hair is short and straight.

2/ They are of medium build.

3/ Albert is overweight.

4/ Mark has a scar above his right eyebrow.

5/ Her facial features are very delicate.

BONUS : *Quelques expressions idiomatiques :*

1/ Il est maigre comme un clou : avoir la peau sur les os.

2/ Avoir un œil au beurre noir : avoir une marque bleue/noire après un coup ou un traumatisme au visage.

3/ Couper les cheveux en quatre : être très pointilleux.

4/ Avoir quelqu'un dans le nez : détester une personne.

5/ Obéir au doigt et à l'œil : obéir sans discuter.

6/ Parler dans sa barbe : parler tout doucement pour que personne n'entende.

Réponses / Answer Key :

*I/5 : « verres de contact » est aussi couramment utilisé.

I	II	III
1/ a	1/ bronzée	1/ le rasoir
2/ b	2/ souple	2/ la vue
3/ c	3/ costaud	3/ la boisson
4/ b	4/ élancée	4/ la croissance
5/ d	5/ grassouillet	5/ la vieillesse

IV
1/ des épaules étroites
2/ un visage laid
3/ des oreilles pointues
4/ un corps malade
5/ des yeux vifs/brillants

V
1/ Elle a les cheveux courts et raides.
2/ Ils/elles sont de taille moyenne.
3/ Albert est en surpoids.
4/ Mark a une cicatrice au-dessus de son arcade sourcilière droite.
5/ Les traits de son visage sont très délicats.

CHAPITRE 4
Les traits de caractère & les émotions /
Personality Traits & Emotions

I/ Choisissez la bonne réponse :

1/ Il a perdu son portefeuille. Il est très _____ .
- a/ heureux
- b/ en colère
- c/ décontracté
- d/ amoureux

2/ Quand je suis à la plage, je suis _____ .
- a/ détendue
- b/ fatiguée
- c/ soucieuse
- d/ nerveuse

3/ Caroline a oublié un rendez-vous important. Elle est ___.
- a/ enduite
- b/ ennuyante
- c/ ennuyée
- d/ ennuie

4/ Mon chat se couche toujours sur mes genoux. Il est _____.
- a/ affublé
- b/ affecté
- c/ affairé
- d/ affectueux

5/ J'adore ma cousine qui est très ____ quand je suis triste.
- a/ indifférente
- b/ déprimante
- c/ méprisante
- d/ réconfortante

II/ Associez les traits de caractère suivants à leur définition :

a/ la sensibilité	b/ l'amabilité	c/ la timidité

d/ la compréhension	e/ la méchanceté

1/ _____ : action de faire du mal aux autres.

2/ _____ : ne pas se sentir à l'aise en public.

3/ _____ : comprendre les difficultés des autres.

4/ _____ : être touché par un évènement ou une personne.

5/ _____ : le fait d'être agréable envers quelqu'un.

III/ Éliminez l'intrus :

1/ énervé/fâché/en colère/agacé/heureux

2/ blasé/étonné/surpris/stupéfait/déconcerté

3/ jaloux/tolérant/envieux/exclusif/possessif

4/ ému/attendri/distant/touché/troublé

5/ inquiet/soucieux/sur le qui-vive/rassuré/tourmenté

IV/ Associez l'adjectif qui correspond le mieux aux émotions des personnes suivantes :

a/ fier(ère)	b/ maladroit(e)	c/ sensible

d/ contrarié(e)	e/ égoïste

1/ _____ : Karine a raté son concours d'entrée.

2/ _____ : Sophie n'aime pas regarder des films d'horreur.

3/ _____ : Grégoire renverse toujours son verre d'eau.

4/ _____ : Marie a obtenu son diplôme avec mention.

5/ _____ : Aditi ne veut pas partager son gâteau.

V/ *Traduisez les phrases suivantes :*

1/ She's angry because she missed her bus.

2/ We're disappointed that we can't go on vacation.

3/ Do you really trust them?

4/ I'm always in a good mood in the morning.

5/ They can't stand rude people.

BONUS : *Quelques expressions idiomatiques :*

1/ Broyer du noir : être déprimé

2/ Voir la vie en rose : être optimiste

3/ Se lever du pied gauche : être de mauvaise humeur dès le matin quand on se lève.

4/ Avoir une peur bleue : être très effrayé par quelque chose.

5/ Être malheureux comme les pierres : être extrêmement malheureux

Réponses / Answer Key:

I	II	III	IV
1/ b	1/ e	1/ heureux	1/ d
2/ a	2/ c	2/ blasé	2/ c
3/ c	3/ d	3/ tolérant	3/ b
4/ d	4/ a	4/ distant	4/ a
5/ d	5/ b	5/ rassuré	5/ e

V
1/ Elle est en colère parce qu'elle a raté/manqué son bus.
2/ Nous sommes déçus de ne pas pouvoir partir en vacances.
3/ Leur faites-vous/Est-ce que vous leur faites vraiment confiance?
4/ Je suis toujours de bonne humeur le matin.
5/ Ils ne supportent pas les gens grossiers/impolis.

CHAPITRE 5

**Les membres de la famille & les réunions familiales /
Family Members & Family Gatherings**

I/ *Choisissez la bonne réponse :*

1/ La mère de ma mère, c'est ma _____.

    a/ belle-mère
    b/ marraine
    c/ tante
    d/ grand-mère

2/ Le fils de ma sœur, c'est mon _____.

    a/ neveu
    b/ nièce
    c/ cousin
    d/ beau-fils

3/ Le mari de ma fille, c'est mon _____.

    a/ cousin
    b/ neveu
    c/ oncle
    d/ gendre

4/ Le père de ma femme, c'est mon _____.

    a/ oncle
    b/ cousin germain
    c/ beau-père
    d/ grand-père

5/ La sœur de ma grand-mère, c'est ma _____.

    a/ grand-tante
    b/ grande tante
    c/ grande cousine
    d/ arrière-grand-tante

II/ À quelle réunion familiale correspondent les situations suivantes :

a/ un mariage	b/ un enterrement	c/ une naissance

d/ un anniversaire	e/ un anniversaire de mariage

1/ _____ : Fatima va épouser l'amour de sa vie.

2/ _____ : ce jeune couple vient d'avoir un bébé.

3/ _____ : ils sont mariés depuis 50 ans.

4/ _____ : cet homme est décédé.

5/ _____ : il y a vingt bougies sur ce gâteau au chocolat.

III/ Associez les mots suivants à leur définition :

a/ le foyer	b/ des demi-sœurs	c/ des jumeaux

d/ homoparentale	e/ une compagne

1/ _____ : elle vit en couple sans être mariée.

2/ _____ : une famille de deux pères ou de deux mères.

3/ _____ : la maison ou une unité familiale.

4/ _____ : elles ont un parent en commun.

5/ _____ : deux frères qui se ressemblent comme deux gouttes d'eau.

IV/ Masculin ou féminin :

1/ jumelle : _____	6/ funérailles : _____
2/ copine : _____	7/ divorce : _____
3/ orphelin : _____	8/ réconciliation : _____
4/ adoption : _____	9/ livret de famille : _____
5/ couple : _____	10/ dispute : _____

V/ Éliminez l'intrus :

1/ un divorce/un mariage/des fiançailles/une union civile/un concubinage

2/ un copain/un ami/un collègue/un concurrent/un compagnon

3/ un mari/une femme/un amant/un orphelin/une fiancée

4/ détester/ admirer/mépriser/haïr/exécrer

5/ une invitation/une offre/une requête/une convocation/une annulation

BONUS : Citations Littéraires :

1/ « Une famille est un ensemble de gens qui se défendent en bloc et s'attaquent en particulier. » Diane de Beausacq, Artiste, Écrivaine (1829-1890).

2/ « Le mariage c'est résoudre à deux les problèmes qu'on n'aurait pas eus tout seul. » Sacha Guitry, Acteur, Artiste, Cinéaste, Scénariste (1885-19570).

3/ « Les grandes personnes ne comprennent jamais rien toutes seules, et c'est fatigant, pour les enfants, de toujours et toujours leur donner des explications. » Antoine de Saint-Exupéry, Artiste, Aviateur, Écrivain (1900-1944).

Réponses / Answer Key :

I	II	III	IV	
1/ d	1/ a	1/ e	1/ F	6/ F
2/ a	2/ c	2/ d	2/ F	7/ M
3/ d	3/ e	3/ a	3/ M	8/ F
4/ c	4/ b	4/ b	4/ F	9/ M
5/ a	5/ d	5/ c	5/ M	10/ F

V		
1/ un divorce	2/ un concurrent	3/ un orphelin
4/ admirer	5/ une annulation	

CHAPITRE 6

L'alimentation & la cuisine / Food & Cooking

I/ Choisissez la bonne réponse :

1/ Sur la table, il y a _____.
 a/ une serviette/un tapis/une soucoupe
 b/ une serviette/un placard/une tasse
 c/ une serviette/une tasse/un couteau
 d/ une serviette/un lave-vaisselle/un verre

2/ Les assiettes sont sales. Mets-les dans le _____.
 a/ réfrigérateur
 b/ grille-pain
 c/ lave-vaisselle
 d/ four

3/ Pour cuire un poulet, on peut le mettre _____.
 a/ au four
 b/ dans un grille-pain
 c/ au frigo
 d/ dans l'évier

4/ Les aliments naturels et sans pesticides sont _____.
 a/ bioniques
 b/ biosphériques
 c/ biologiques
 d/ biodynamiques

5/ Pour égoutter des légumes, on utilise _____.
 a/ une passoire
 b/ une mangeoire
 c/ un grimoire
 d/ un prétoire

II/ Éliminez l'intrus :

1/ des citrons/des clémentines/des kumquats/des poires/des mandarines

2/ un poireau/un navet/une prune/un artichaut/un chou

3/ de la bière/du vin blanc/du soda/du champagne/du whisky

4/ une carafe/un verre/une tasse/un fouet/une bouteille

5/ une palourde/une huître/une crevette/un bulot/un œuf

III/ Masculin ou féminin :

1/ grillade : _____	6/ olive : _____
2/ riz : _____	7/ brioche : _____
3/ courgette : _____	8/ pastèque : _____
4/ noyau : _____	9/ vinaigrette : _____
5/ champignon : _____	10/ régime : _____

IV/ Associez les mots suivants à leur définition :

a/ un régime	b/ des surgelés	c/ des agrumes
d/ des fruits de mer	e/ épicé	

1/ _____ : un plat préparé avec des piments.

2/ _____ : la sélection stricte d'aliments spécifiques.

3/ _____ : des fruits acides qui contiennent beaucoup de jus.

4/ _____ : des aliments que l'on conserve au congélateur.

5/ _____ : on en trouve dans les mers ou les océans.

V/ Composez le menu d'un repas complet. Deux choix sont possibles par catégorie :

a/ un mille-feuille	f/ un diabolo menthe	k/ du reblochon
b/ des haricots verts	g/ des coquilles Saint-Jacques	l/ un panaché
c/ du camembert	h/ un demi-panaché	m/ une crème caramel
d/ une grillade de poulet	i/ un œuf dur mayonnaise	
e/ des rondelles de concombre	j/ du riz	

1/ L'entrée : _____.

2/ Le plat principal complet : _____.

3/ Le fromage : _____.

4/ Le dessert : _____.

5/ La boisson : _____.

BONUS : Quelques expressions idiomatiques :

1/ Manger sur le pouce : manger rapidement.

2/ Être un vrai cordon bleu : être un/une excellent(e) cuisinier/cuisinière.

3/ Ne pas être dans son assiette : ne pas se sentir bien.

4/ Mettre du beurre dans les épinards : améliorer sa situation financière.

5/ Acheter quelque chose pour une bouchée de pain : acheter quelque chose très bon marché.

Réponses / Answer Key :

I	II	III		IV
1/ c	1/ des poires	1/ F	6/ F	1/ e
2/ c	2/ une prune	2/ M	7/ F	2/ a
3/ a	3/ du soda	3/ F	8/ F	3/ c
4/ c	4/ un fouet	4/ M	9/ F	4/ b
5/ a	5/ un œuf	5/ M	10/ M	5/ d

V
1/ L'entrée : des rondelles de concombre ou un œuf dur mayonnaise
2/ Le plat principal complet : 1/ une grillade de poulet avec des haricots verts 2/ des coquilles Saint-Jacques avec du riz 3/ une grillade de poulet avec du riz 4/ des coquilles Saint-Jacques avec des haricots verts.
3/ Le fromage : du camembert ou du reblochon
4/ Le dessert : un mille-feuille ou une crème caramel
5/ La boisson : un diabolo menthe ou un panaché

CHAPITRE 7

La santé/ Health

I/ Choisissez la bonne réponse :

1/ J'ai trop mangé de chocolat. Je/j'_____.
    a/ me sens en forme
    b/ ai la nausée
    c/ suis en bonne santé
    d/ ai mal aux pieds

2/ Elle tousse beaucoup parce qu'elle a mal _____.
    a/ au pied
    b/ au cou
    c/ à la gorge
    d/ au nez

3/ Je dois me faire opérer de l'appendicite alors j'ai pris rendez-vous chez une _____.
    a/ vaurienne
    b/ épicurienne
    c/ obstétricienne
    d/ chirurgienne

4/ La pneumonie est une maladie qui touche les _____.
    a/ intestins
    b/ poumons
    c/ reins
    d/ os

5/ Après avoir fait un jogging d'une heure, j'ai des _____.
    a/ courbatures
    b/ courgettes
    c/ conjonctures
    d/ vergetures

II/ Éliminez l'intrus :

1/ une infirmière/une pneumologue/une vendeuse/une aide-soignante/un médecin

2/ un pied/une cheville/un mollet/un orteil/une oreille

3/ se relever/s'évanouir/tomber/glisser/déraper

4/ un cachet/un sirop/une gélule/une pastille/une capsule

5/ le nez/la bouche/la jambe/le front/les joues

III/ Associez les mots suivants à leur définition :

a/ du sang	b/ une piqûre	c/ guérir
d/ le SAMU		e/ une ordonnance

1/ _____ : c'est le service des soins médicaux d'urgence.

2/ _____ : on vous en fait une pour vous vacciner.

3/ _____ : nous en avons entre 4 et 6 litres dans le corps.

4/ _____ : c'est l'objectif du personnel médical.

5/ _____ : une liste de médicaments que vous prescrit un médecin.

IV/ Complétez les phrases avec les mots suivants :

a/ enceinte	b/ une radio	c/ tension artérielle
d/ un pansement		e/ la grippe

1/ Il faudrait passer _____ pour savoir si tu t'es cassé le bras.

2/ Elle attend un heureux évènement. Elle est _____.

3/ Il est cardiaque donc il doit surveiller sa _____.

4/ Elle a beaucoup de fièvre donc elle a peut-être _____.

5/ Je me suis coupée. Donne-moi _____, s'il te plaît.

V/ *Traduisez les phrases suivantes :*

1/ I have a sore throat and I have a runny nose.

2/ She just sprained her ankle playing tennis.

3/ We have a dentist's appointment tomorrow morning.

4/ If she does not get enough sleep, she gets headaches.

5/ I have been sneezing a lot because I have allergies.

BONUS : *Quelques expressions idiomatiques :*

1/ Casser sa pipe/passer l'arme à gauche : mourir.

2/ Reprendre du poil de la bête : se rétablir après une maladie.

3/ Tomber dans les pommes/tourner de l'œil : s'évanouir.

4/ Avoir une fièvre de cheval : avoir énormément de fièvre.

5/ Jeter un œil : regarder rapidement quelque chose.

Réponses / Answer Key :

I	II	III	IV
1/ b	1/ une vendeuse	1/ d	1/ b
2/ c	2/ une oreille	2/ b	2/ a
3/ d	3/ se relever	3/ a	3/ c
4/ b	4/ un sirop	4/ c	4/ e
5/ a	5/ la jambe	5/ e	5/ d

V
1/ J'ai mal à la gorge et j'ai le nez qui coule.
2/ Elle vient de se fouler la cheville en jouant au tennis.
3/ Nous avons (un) rendez-vous chez le dentiste demain matin.
4/ Si elle ne dort pas assez, elle a des maux de tête.
5/ J'éternue beaucoup parce que j'ai des allergies.

CHAPITRE 8

La maison & le mobilier / The House & The Furniture

I/ Choisissez la bonne réponse :

1/ Dans une salle de bains, il y a _____.

    a/ un évier
    b/ un lavabo
    c/ un abreuvoir
    d/ un bassin

2/ Nous gardons tous nos vieux meubles _____.

    a/ sur le toit
    b/ dans les toilettes
    c/ dans la salle de bains
    d/ au grenier

3/ Elle n'aime pas monter les escaliers alors elle habite_____.

    a/ au rez-de-chaussée
    b/ au sous-sol
    c/ sur le palier
    d/ au dernier étage

4/ Quand je me réveille, j'ai mal au dos alors je dois changer _____.

    a/ les draps
    b/ la couette
    c/ le matelas
    d/ le couvre-lit

5/ Avant d'entrer chez quelqu'un, on appuie sur _____.

    a/ la sornette
    b/ la sonnette
    c/ la buvette
    d/ la disette

II/ Éliminez l'intrus :

1/ un canapé/une chaise/un tabouret/une armoire/un fauteuil

2/ emménager/s'installer/déménager/s'établir/se fixer

3/ un logement/un jardin/une habitation/un logis/une demeure

4/ le loyer/le plafond/le sol/le mur/le toit

5/ des lits/des étagères/des buffets/des placards/des penderies

III/ Vrai ou faux ? Quand c'est faux, indiquez la réponse correcte :

1/ __ : un locataire possède son logement.

_____.

2/ __ : le loyer est une somme d'argent pour payer un logement.

_____ .

3/ ___ : une cour est un espace ouvert au milieu des immeubles.

_____ .

4/ ___ : un logement bruyant est très agréable.

_____ .

5/ ___ : on utilise la climatisation en hiver.

_____.

IV/ Quelle utilisation faites-vous des éléments suivants?

a/ une table basse	b/ une couette	c/ un oreiller
d/ un lavabo		e/ un aspirateur

1/ _____ : on y dispose des verres ou des tasses.

2/ _____ : on peut s'y laver les mains.

3/ _____ : elle tient chaud pendant les nuits d'hiver.

4/ _____ : il est utile pour faire le ménage.

5/ _____ : il permet de dormir plus confortablement.

V/ *Traduisez les phrases suivantes :*

1/ We bought two leather armchairs.

2/ I would like to rent a three-bedroom apartment.

3/ She needs to buy curtains and two carpets.

4/ He lives on the third floor in this old building.

5/ I have an appointment with a real estate agent.

BONUS : *Quelques expressions idiomatiques :*

1/ Mener la vie de château : mener une vie aisée, sans avoir de difficultés financières.

2/ Parler à un mur : parler à une personne qui n'est pas touchée par ce que vous dites.

3/ Sauter au plafond : une réaction qui trahit une surprise extrême.

4/ Prendre la porte : quitter une pièce (sous la contrainte/en colère) / quitter un emploi.

Réponses / *Answer Key :*

I	II	III	IV
1/ b	1/ une armoire	1/ F - un/une propriétaire	1/ a
2/ d	2/ déménager	2/ V	2/ d
3/ a	3/ un jardin	3/ V	3/ b
4/ c	4/ le loyer	4/ F - au calme, paisible	4/ e
5/ b	5/ des lits	5/ F - le chauffage	5/ c

V
1/ Nous avons acheté deux fauteuils en cuir.
2/ Je voudrais louer un appartement de trois pièces.
3/ Elle a besoin d'acheter des rideaux et deux tapis.
4/ Il habite au troisième étage dans ce vieil immeuble.
5/ J'ai (un) rendez-vous avec un agent immobilier.

CHAPITRE 9

La ville & la campagne / City Life & Country Life

I/ *Choisissez la bonne réponse :*

1/ On m'a volé mon portefeuille, je dois aller _____
  a/ à la gare
  b/ au centre des impôts
  c/ au commissariat
  d/ à la mairie

2/ On cultive du blé dans _____
  a/ un verger
  b/ un maraîcher
  c/ un jardin
  d/ un champ

3/ Le bétail, c'est _____
  a/ une machine agricole
  b/ une grande porte
  c/ l'ensemble des bêtes d'élevage (vaches, moutons, etc.)
  d/ une spécialité culinaire du nord de la France.

4/ Les villes de Paris et de Marseille sont divisées en_____
  a/ arrondissements
  b/ ronds-points
  c/ ruelles
  d/ régions

5/ Je veux envoyer cette lettre. Où se trouve _____, s'il vous plaît ?
  a/ le poste
  b/ le bureau
  c/ la poste
  d/ le courrier

II/ Éliminez l'intrus :

1/ un musée/un opéra/un cinéma/un camping/un théâtre

2/ un pré/un champ/un verger/une vigne/un immeuble

3/ urbain/rural/campagnard/naturel/biologique

4/ le maïs/le blé/le pain/l'orge/le houblon

5/ cultiver/récolter/faire pousser/semer/arracher

III/ L'écologie : Déterminez si les actions suivantes sont bonnes ou mauvaises pour l'environnement :

a/ jeter des sacs dans la nature	b/ faire du vélo	c/ extraire de plus en plus de charbon

d/ recycler les plastiques	e/ prendre des douches plus courtes

Bonnes pour l'environnement : _____

Mauvaises pour l'environnement : _____

IV/ Associez les mots suivants à leur définition :

a/ le gaz à effet de serre	b/ des ordures	c/ un gendarme

d/ une agricultrice	e/ un gaspillage

1/ _____ : ce sont des déchets que l'on jette à la poubelle.

2/ _____ : une consommation inutile d'argent ou alimentaire

3/ _____ : elle travaille sur une exploitation agricole.

4/ _____ : il représente un danger pour la planète

5/ _____ : c'est un militaire qui assure la sécurité publique.

V/ Traduisez les phrases suivantes :

1/ Pedestrians must watch out when crossing the streets.

2/ We visited wonderful vineyards in the South of France.

3/ Large intersections and many roundabouts are found in several cities.

4/ Sheep, goats, cows, and pigs are farm animals.

5/ On a hot summer day, there are often flies, mosquitoes, and wasps.

BONUS : Quelques expressions idiomatiques :

1/ Avoir la main verte : savoir entretenir et faire pousser des plantes

2/ Faire quelque chose en coup de vent : faire quelque chose très rapidement

3/ Couper l'herbe sous les pieds de quelqu'un : empêcher un concurrent de progresser ou le devancer

4/ Regarder les mouches voler : ne rien faire du tout.

Réponses / Answer Key :

I	II	III	IV
1/ c	1/ un camping	Bonnes : b	1/ b
2/ d	2/ un immeuble	d	2/ e
3/ c	3/ urbain	e	3/ d
4/ a	4/ le pain	Mauvaises : a	4/ a
5/ c	5/ arracher	c	5/ c

V
1/ Les piétons doivent faire attention avant de traverser la rue.
2/ Nous avons visité des vignobles merveilleux dans le sud de la France.
3/ On trouve de grands carrefours et beaucoup de ronds-points dans plusieurs villes.
4/ Les moutons, les chèvres, les vaches, et les cochons sont des animaux de ferme.
5/ Pendant une chaude journée d'été, il y a souvent des mouches, des moustiques et des guêpes.

CHAPITRE 10

L'habillement & la mode / Clothing & Fashion

I/ Choisissez la bonne réponse :

1/ Quand j'ai froid aux mains, je mets des _____.
- a/ écharpes
- b/ gants
- c/ collants
- d/ chaussettes

2/ Ton pantalon est trop grand, tu devrais mettre _____.
- a/ un fil
- b/ une sangle
- c/ une cordelette
- d/ une ceinture

3/ Cette robe n'est pas moderne. Elle est _____
- a/ démodée
- b/ bouchée
- c/ démoulée
- d/ démotivée

4/ Pendant les _____, on peut faire de bonnes affaires.
- a/ avantages
- b/ réductions
- c/ soldes
- d/ occasions

5/ Pour savoir si un vêtement vous va avant de l'acheter, vous allez dans _____ d'essayage.
- a/ un cabanon
- b/ une cabane
- c/ une cahute
- d/ une cabine

II/ Associez les mots suivants à leur définition :

a/ un imperméable	b/ un foulard	c/ une blouse

d/ un blouson	e/ des pantoufles

1/ _____ : il tient chaud quand on fait de la moto.

2/ _____ : un médecin en porte une pour protéger ses vêtements.

3/ _____ : c'est un accessoire favori des Parisiennes.

4/ _____ : il vous protège quand il pleut.

5/ _____ : nous les mettons quand nous rentrons chez nous.

III/ Masculin ou féminin :

1/ peignoir : ____	6/ cravate : _____
2/ chaussettes : ____	7/ chapeau : ____
3/ anorak : ____	8/ pantoufles : _____
4/ bottes : ____	9/ soutien-gorge : _____
5/ bermuda : _____	10/ collants : _____

IV/ Quels vêtements choisir parmi cette liste pour assister aux évènements suivants ?

a/ une robe longue	b/ un maillot de bain	c/ un costume

d/ une salopette	e/ un survêtement

1/ _____ : un pique-nique à la plage

2/ _____ : un entretien professionnel

3/ _____ : un jogging dans un parc

4/ _____ : repeindre une maison

5/ _____ : un mariage élégant

V/ Traduisez les phrases suivantes :

1/ I bought this shirt in a department store.

2/ Don't forget to bring a jacket!

3/ They like to wear linen clothes in the summer.

4/ These boots are made for walking in the snow.

5/ This pair of pants looks good on you.

BONUS : Quelques expressions idiomatiques :

1/ Faire du lèche-vitrine : regarder les vitrines des magasins sans y entrer et sans rien y acheter.

2/ Retourner sa veste : changer de camp dans une situation précise.

3/ Se serrer la ceinture : être obligé de faire des économies pour survivre.

4/ Aller comme un gant à quelqu'un : être à la bonne taille.

Réponses / Answer Key :

I	II	III		IV
1/ b	1/ d	1/ M	6/ F	1/ b
2/ d	2/ c	2/ F	7/ M	2/ c
3/ a	3/ b	3/ M	8/ F	3/ e
4/ c	4/ a	4/ F	9/ M	4/ d
5/ d	5/ e	5/ M	10/ M	5/ a

V
1/ J'ai acheté cette chemise dans un grand magasin.
2/ N' oublie pas/n' oubliez pas d'apporter une veste!
3/ Ils aiment porter/mettre des vêtements en lin en été.
4/ Ces bottes sont faites pour marcher dans la neige.
5/ Ce pantalon vous va bien.

CHAPITRE 11

Les études & la formation / Studies & Training

I/ Choisissez la bonne réponse :

1/ Sophie doit _____ un examen de fin d'année.
a/ subir
b/ prendre
c/ passer
d/ s'asseoir

2/ Fatima veut faire des _____ de chimie et de physique.
a/ étudies
b/ étudiant
c/ étudier
d/ études

3/ Augustine a obtenu de bonnes _____ ce semestre.
a/ degrés
b/ grades
c/ notes
d/ résultats

4/ Après leurs études, les étudiants font souvent _____
a/ un stagiaire
b/ un stage
c/ un cours
d/ une période

5/ Priyanka va habiter dans _____ universitaire à la rentrée.
a/ une cité
b/ un immeuble
c/ un village
d/ un hameau

II/ Éliminez l'intrus :

1/ un stagiaire/un apprenti/un musicien/un élève/un lycéen

2/ la physique/la chimie/l'espagnol/la géométrie/l'algèbre

3/ un examen/un cahier/un quiz /une épreuve/un concours

4/ le musée/le lycée/la maternelle/l'école primaire/la fac

5/ étudier/réviser/apprendre/approfondir/s'amuser

III/ Complétez les phrases avec les mots proposés :

a/ resto U	b/ un crayon	c/ les devoirs
d/ tricher		e/ la conférence

1/ C'est toujours une mauvaise idée de _____ à un examen.

2/ Je n'ai pas pu assister à _____ d'hier matin.

3/ Elle n'a pas de stylo mais elle peut te prêter _____.

4/ J'ai faim. Viens avec moi au _____.

5/ ___ que nous a donnés Madame Bernard étaient difficiles.

IV/ Masculin ou féminin :

1/ erreur :____	6/ apprentissage :___
2/ trimestre :____	7/ cours :___
3/ cahier :____	8/ compétence :___
4/ licence :____	9/ baccalauréat :___
5/ résultat:___	10/ maternelle : ___

V/ Associez la matière scolaire la plus appropriée pour exercer les professions suivantes :

a/ l'informatique	b/ l'anthropologie	c/ la biologie
d/ la botanique		e/ les relations internationales

1/ un ambassadeur/ambassadrice (diplomatie) :

_____

2/ un/une archéologue :

_____

3/ un médecin :

4/ un jardinier :

5/ un ingénieur/une ingénieure :

BONUS : Quelques expressions idiomatiques :

1/ Avoir la bosse de(s) : avoir des dispositions naturelles pour apprendre une matière scientifique (les maths, la physique, etc.)

2/ Étudier le terrain : observer la situation avant d'agir

BONUS : Citations Littéraires :

1/ « Enseigner, ce n'est pas remplir un vase, c'est allumer un feu. » Michel de Montaigne, Écrivain français (1533-1592)

2/ « Qui ne continue pas à apprendre est indigne d'enseigner. » Gaston Bachelard, Philosophe français (1884-1962)

3/ « Je n'ai jamais rien étudié, mais tout vécu et cela m'a appris quelque chose. » Antonin Artaud, Écrivain français (1896-1948).

Réponses/Answer Key :

I	II	III	IV		V
1/ c	1/ un musicien	1/ d	1/ F	6/ M	1/ e
2/ d	2/ l'espagnol	2/ e	2/ M	7/ M	2/ b
3/ c	3/ un cahier	3/ b	3/ M	8/ F	3/ c
4/ b	4/ le musée	4/ a	4/ F	9/ M	4/ d
5/ a	5/ s'amuser	5/ c	5/ M	10/ F	5/ a

CHAPITRE 12

Les transports / Transportation

I/ Choisissez la bonne réponse :

1/ Il est difficile de rouler dans Paris à cause _____
   a/ des capsules
   b/ des embouts
   c/ du co-voiturage
   d/ des embouteillages

2/ A quel étage du terminal se trouvent _____ ?
   a/ les départements
   b/ les départs
   c/ les allers
   d/ les allées

3/ Mohamed travaille pour Air France. Il est _____ .
   a/ garçon
   b/ serveur
   c/ steward
   d/ chef de rang

4/ Le train _____ de Paris entrera en gare dans cinq minutes.
   a/ en provenance
   b/ provient de
   c/ arrivé
   d/ qui roule

5/ Madame, vous devez acheter un autre billet. Celui-ci n'est plus _____ .
   a/ bien
   b/ actuel
   c/ exploitable
   d/ valable

II/ Trouvez le contraire des mots suivants :

1/ décoller : _____ .

2/ avoir de l'avance : _____ .

3/ accélérer : _____ .

4/ les départs : _____ .

5/ allumer les phares : _____ .

III/ Associez les métiers suivants à leur définition :

a/ un bagagiste	b/ un agent d'escale	c/ un billet aller-retour
d/ la gare routière		e/ le personnel navigant

1/ _____ : il enregistre vos bagages et vous donne votre carte d'embarquement.

2/ _____ : il met vos valises dans la soute de l'avion.

3/ _____ : vous y prenez un autobus ou un autocar.

4/ _____ : il vous permet de faire un voyage complet.

5/ _____ : il est chargé de rendre votre voyage plus sûr et agréable.

IV/ Masculin ou féminin :

1/ vélo:_____	6/ tarif:_____
2/ stationnement:_____	7/ équipage:_____
3/ excès de vitesse:_____	8/ douane:_____
4/ embarquement:_____	9/ trajet:_____
5/ terminus:_____	10/ station:_____

V/ Complétez les phrases avec les mots suivants :

a/ l'autoroute	b/ un pneu	c/ en sens interdit

d/ composter	e/ bagage à main

1/ Marc est pressé alors il va prendre _____ .

2/ On a droit à un _____ dans la cabine d'un avion.

3/ N'oubliez pas de _____ votre billet de train.

4/ Sophie va dans un garage pour réparer _____ crevé.

5/ Ne tourne pas à gauche ! La rue est _____ .

BONUS : Quelques expressions idiomatiques :

1/ Appuyer sur le champignon : accélérer pendant que vous conduisez.

2/ Arriver à bon port : arriver quelque part sans accident.

3/ Griller un feu rouge : ne pas s'arrêter à un feu rouge.

4/ Faire le plein : remplir complètement votre réservoir d'essence.

Réponses / Answer Key :

I	II	III	IV		V
1/ d	1/ atterrir	1/ b	1/ M	6/ M	1/ a
2/ b	2/ avoir du retard	2/ a	2/ M	7/ M	2/ e
3/ c	3/ ralentir	3/ d	3/ M	8/ F	3/ d
4/ a	4/ les arrivées	4/ c	4/ M	9/ M	4/ b
5/ d	5/ éteindre les phares	5/ e	5/ M	10/ F	5/ c

CHAPITRE 13

Le cinéma & la télévision

I/ Choisissez la bonne réponse :

1/ Je voudrais prendre une photo, prête-moi _____, s'il te plaît ?

    a/ ton camescope
    b/ ton appareil-photo
    c/ ta caméra
    d/ ton appareillage

2/ Ce journaliste politique va faire_____ sur le président ce soir à la télé.

    a/ un rapport
    b/ une diffusion
    c/ un report
    d/ un reportage

3/ ___ de ce film a reçu deux prix au Festival de Cannes.

    a/ Le réalisateur
    b/ Le gérant
    c/ La direction
    d/ Le directeur

4/ J'adore regarder _____ littéraires et de variétés à la télé.

    a/ les omissions
    b/ les programmations
    c/ les émissions
    d/ les admissions

5/ Ce film d'action est projeté sur _____ en 3D.

    a/ un écran
    b/ un film
    c/ une toile
    d/ un voile

II/ Éliminez l'intrus :

1/ une actrice/une comédienne/une tragédienne/une figurante/ une productrice

2/ une histoire/un décor/une intrigue/un roman/un scénario

3/ l'éclairage/une ampoule/une lampe/un fauteuil/un luminaire

4/ muet/bruyant/silencieux/discret/réservé

5/ un festival/un tournage/une caméra/une prise de vue/une réalisation

III/ Trouvez le contraire des adjectifs suivants :

1/ amusant : _____.

2/ médiocre : _____.

3/ tragique : _____.

4/ insolent : _____.

5/ terrifiant : _____ .

IV/ Associez les mots suivants à leur définition :

a/ une bande-annonce	b/ un monteur	c/ une habilleuse
d/ une cascadeuse		e/ un entracte

1/ _____ : il assemble les plans et les séquences d'un film.

2/ _____ : elle crée ou choisit les costumes des acteurs.

3/ _____ : elle incite les gens à aller voir des films.

4/ _____ : une courte interruption dans un spectacle.

5/ _____ : elle remplace une actrice dans une scène dangereuse.

V/ Déterminez le genre de film décrit dans les résumés des cinq films suivants :

a/ horreur	b/ comédie	c/ fantastique

d/ dessin animé	e/ film d'action

1/ _____ : une princesse danoise possède le pouvoir magique de tout transformer en glace.

2/ _____ : un parc d'attraction avec des animaux préhistoriques.

3/ _____ : un homme fou harcèle ses victimes sur une île déserte.

4/ _____ : un espion est poursuivi par de dangereux criminels à Paris.

5/ _____ : des amis se retrouvent dans un club de vacances en Espagne.

BONUS : Quelques expressions idiomatiques :

En faire tout un cinéma : donner une importance excessive à quelque chose.
Arrête de faire ton cinéma! : arrête de faire semblant !

BONUS : Citations de personnalités du cinéma :

1/ « Le cinéma, c'est une dépendance, mais elle est tellement agréable que le plaisir l'emporte sur les mauvaises raisons, comme le besoin de fuir la réalité. » Isabelle Huppert, Actrice (1953-)

2/ « Le cinéma, c'est l'écriture moderne dont l'encre est la lumière » Jean Cocteau, Écrivain et Cinéaste (1889-1963)

Réponses / Answer Key :

I	II
1/ b	1/ une productrice
2/ d	2/ un décor
3/ a	3/ un fauteuil
4/ c	4/ bruyant
5/ a	5/ un festival

III
1/ ennuyeux, assommant, embêtant
2/ excellent, brillant, grandiose
3/ comique, burlesque, léger
4/ poli, respectueux, modeste
5/ rassurant, apaisant, réconfortant

IV	V
1/ b	1/ d
2/ c	2/ c
3/ a	3/ a
4/ e	4/ e
5/ d	5/ b

CHAPITRE 14

La presse, la radio & l'internet /
The Press, the Radio & the Internet

I/ *Choisissez la bonne réponse :*

1/ Voici le document que tu dois _____ sur ton ordinateur.

    a/ charger
    b/ télécharger
    c/ recharger
    d/ télécopier

2/ Un journal publié tous les jours est _____

    a/ un hebdomadaire
    b/ un mensuel
    c/ un quotidien
    d/ un trimestriel

3/ La personne responsable de tous les journalistes d'un journal ou d'un magazine est _____

    a/ le chef
    b/ le gérant
    c/ l'éditeur
    d/ le rédacteur en chef

4/ Les personnes qui écoutent la radio sont _____

    a/ des lecteurs
    b/ des auditeurs
    c/ des spectateurs
    d/ des internautes

5/ Je ne peux plus taper sur _____. Je crois qu'il est bloqué.

    a/ mon écritoire
    b/ mon clavier
    c/ mon tableau de clés
    d/ mon tableau de bord

II/ *Éliminez l'intrus :*

1/ un présentateur/un animateur/un commentateur/un auteur/un annonceur

2/ un magazine/un périodique/un bulletin/une gazette/un entretien

3/ une correspondante/une journaliste/une reporter/une envoyée spéciale/une avocate

4/ une boîte aux lettres/un podcast/une messagerie/une boîte postale/une adresse électronique

5/ une corde/un lien/une ficelle/un cordon/un boulon

III/ *Associez les mots suivants à leur définition :*

a/ un sondage	b/ une version numérique	c/ une enquête
d/ un fait divers		e/ une souris

1/ _____ : elle vous permet de naviguer sur l'écran d'un ordinateur.

2/ _____ : certains journaux et magazines en proposent une que l'on peut lire sur un portable.

3/ _____ : c'est un évènement plus ou moins important.

4/ _____ : c'est une recherche de renseignements sur un sujet particulier.

5/ _____ : c'est une méthode statistique qui sonde l'opinion publique.

IV/ *Masculin ou féminin : Un des mots ci-dessous peut être soit masculin ou féminin selon le sens :*

1/ micro : ___	6/ actualités : _____
2/ clé USB _____	7/ moteur de recherche : _____
3/ publicité : _____	8/ rubrique : _____
4/ tirage : _____	9/ abonnement : _____
5/ réseau social : ___	10/ chronique : _____

V/ Classez les nouvelles suivantes dans leurs rubriques respectives :

a/ les sports	b/ la politique internationale	c/ l'économie

d/ la culture	e/ la météo

1/ _____ : on annonce de fortes pluies dans la soirée.

2/ _____ : la finale du tournoi de tennis a été annulée.

3/ _____ : le musée sur les peintres impressionnistes sera inauguré le 3 juillet.

4/ _____ : les banques européennes ont décidé d'accorder un prêt à l'Argentine.

5/ _____ : la prochaine réunion des chefs d'états d'Amérique Latine aura lieu à Lima au Pérou.

NOTE : un « canard » désigne familièrement un journal. Au XVIème siècle, cela signifiait une fausse nouvelle.

BONUS : Citations de personnalités du monde de la télévision, de la radio et de l'internet :

1/ « Vous allez à la télévision pour éteindre votre cerveau. Vous allez à l'ordinateur lorsque vous voulez activer votre cerveau. » Steve Jobs, Fondateur de Apple (1955-2011)

2/ « La télévision est un spectacle. C'est une tribune, une scène, un journal du monde, un stade, un cirque. » Jean d'Ormesson, Écrivain (1925-2017)

3/ « Tu sais ? Quand tu cherches une rue dans ta voiture, et que tu ne la trouves pas, tu as un réflexe bizarre : tu baisses le son de la radio. » Gad Elmaleh, Acteur, Comique (1971-)

Réponses / Answer Key :

I	II	III	IV		V
1/ b	1/ un auteur	1/ e	1/ M	6/ F	1/ e
2/ c	2/ un entretien	2/ b	2/ F	7/ M	2/ a
3/ d	3/ une avocate	3/ d	3/ F	8/ F	3/ d
4/ b	4/ un podcast	4/ c	4/ M	9/ M	4/ c
5/ b	5/ un boulon	5/ a	5/ M	10/ F	5/ b

CHAPITRE 15

Les arts/ The Arts

I/ Choisissez la bonne réponse :

1/ _____ Rodin au Metropolitan Museum débutera le 3 mai.
  a/ La présentation
  b/ L'exhibition
  c/ L'exposition
  d/ La représentation

2/ Pour peindre, il faut _____ et _____.
  a/ une toile/un cheval
  b/ une pince/un chevalet
  c/ une pincette/une brosse
  d/ un pinceau/un chevalet

3/ J'adore _____ de cette chanson. Elles sont très poétiques.
  a/ le langage
  b/ les mots
  c/ les paroles
  d/ la langue

4/ Au théâtre, tous les acteurs reviennent sur _____ pour saluer le public.
  a/ parquet
  b/ sol
  c/ stage
  d/ scène

5/ J'ai deux _____ pour l'opéra Carmen de Georges Bizet.
  a/ billets
  b/ reçus
  c/ tickets
  d/ récépissés

II/ Éliminez l'intrus :

1/ un poème/un roman/une nouvelle/une pièce/un paysage

2/ un dessin/une estampe/un ballet/un tableau/une esquisse

3/ un musicien/un architecte/un chef d'orchestre/un compositeur/un chansonnier/

4/ une cabane/un manoir/un château/une forteresse/un palais

5/ une galerie/un musée/un débarras/une exposition/une collection

III/ Associez les mots suivants avec leur définition :

a/ une répétition	b/ une cantatrice	c/ l'argile
d/ une nouvelle		e/ des aquarelles

1/ ___ : elle chante des airs d'opéra.

2/ ___ : ce sont des tableaux obtenus grâce à des couleurs transparentes délayées dans l'eau.

3/ ___ : elle vous sert à modeler de la poterie.

4/ ___ : c'est l'étape indispensable avant de jouer un spectacle.

5/ ___ : elle est souvent plus difficile à écrire qu'un roman.

IV/ Associez les artistes suivants à leur domaine artistique respectif :

a/ Vauban	b/ Camille Claudel	c/ Molière
d/ Francoise Sagan		e/ Auguste Renoir

1/ ___ : la peinture

2/ ___ : le théâtre

3/ ___ : la sculpture

4/ ___ : la littérature

5/ ___ : l'architecture militaire

V/ Traduisez les phrases suivantes :

1/ I bought two books at the Louvre gift shop.

2/ The concert was cancelled at the last minute.

3/ The lighting highlights the background of this painting

4/ This circus features the best trapeze act in the world.

5/ Sculptors often choose plaster, marble, or alabaster.

BONUS : Quelques expressions idiomatiques avec les couleurs :

1/ Broyer du noir : être déprimé.

2/ Rire jaune : se forcer à rire.

3/ Voir rouge : être extrêmement en colère.

4/ Être blanc comme neige : être pâle (innocence ou pureté).

5/ Montrer patte blanche : prouver son identité pour entrer dans un endroit.

6/ Donner le feu vert : donner son accord, son autorisation.

7/ Être un vrai cordon bleu : très bien faire la cuisine.

8/ Voir la vie en rose : se montrer optimiste, joyeux.

9/ Se mélanger les pinceaux : ici « pinceaux » veut dire « jambes » : se tromper, ne pas comprendre une situation et agir d'une façon confuse.

BONUS : Citations Littéraires :

1/ « L'art et la parole sont les deux organes du progrès humain. L'un fait communier les cœurs, et l'autre les pensées. » Romain Rolland, Écrivain et Historien de l'art (1866-1944)

2/ « L'artiste doit aimer la vie et nous montrer qu'elle est belle. Sans lui, nous en douterions. » Anatole France, Poète, Journaliste et Romancier (1844-1924)

3/ « Cultivez votre amour de la nature, car c'est la meilleure façon de mieux comprendre l'art. » Vincent Van Gogh, Peintre (1853-1890)

4/ « L'art est fait pour troubler. La science rassure. » Georges

Braque, Peintre, Sculpteur (1882-1963)

Réponses / Answer Key :

I	II	III	IV
1/ c	1/ un paysage	1/ b	1/ e
2/ d	2/ un ballet	2/ e	2/ c
3/ c	3/ un architecte	3/ c	3/ b
4/ d	4/ une cabane	4/ a	4/ d
5/ a	5/ un débarras	5/ d	5/ a

V
1/ J'ai acheté deux livres à la boutique de cadeaux du Louvre.
2/ Le concert a été annulé à la dernière minute.
3/ L'éclairage met en valeur l'arrière-plan de ce tableau.
4/ Ce cirque présente le meilleur numéro de trapèze du monde.
5/ Les sculpteurs choisissent souvent le plâtre, le marbre ou l'albâtre.

CHAPITRE 16

Les jeux & les sports / Games & Sports

I/ Choisissez la bonne réponse :

1/ Elle adore faire du ski alpin. Elle va souvent _____
- a/ à la mer
- b/ à la montagne
- c/ en ville
- d/ au cinéma

2/ Au bord de la mer, mon sport préféré est _____.
- a/ la planche à voile
- b/ la luge
- c/ le ski nordique
- d/ l'escalade

3/ Les deux équipes ont fait _____ .
- a/ match zéro
- b/ le même résultat
- c/ égalité
- d/ match nul

4/ Dans un jeu, il y a toujours _____ et un perdant.
- a/ un profiteur
- b/ à gagner
- c/ en gagnant
- d/ un gagnant

5/ Jules ira commander une pizza pendant _____ du match de football.
- a/ la mi-temps
- b/ le plein-temps
- c/ l'entracte
- d/ l'intervalle

II/ Associez les noms suivants à leur définition :

a/ une randonnée	b/ tricher	c/ des jeux de société
d/ un terrain		e/ en équipe

1/ ___ : c'est une pratique malhonnête dans n'importe quel jeu ou examen.

2/ ___ : le Monopoly, les dames et les dominos.

3/ ___ : on en fait une en montagne ou dans les bois.

4/ ___ : on y joue au football ou au rugby.

5/ ___ : certains sports se pratiquent uniquement de cette manière.

III/ Trouvez le contraire des verbes suivants :

1/ réussir : _____.

2/ s'arrêter : _____.

3/ lancer : _____.

4/ tomber : _____.

5/ soulever : _____.

IV/ De quel jeu ou de quel sport s'agit-il ?

a/ le scrabble	b/ le javelot	c/ les échecs
d/ le waterpolo		e/ l'haltérophilie

1/ ___ : on y joue avec un ballon dans une piscine.

2/ ___ : c'est un jeu qui demande une connaissance de stratégies complexes.

3/ ___ : le but de ce jeu est de composer des mots avec des lettres qui vont vous rapporter le plus de points.

4/ ___ : ces athlètes portent des poids extrêmement lourds.

5/ ___ : pour pratiquer ce sport, il faut avoir beaucoup de force dans un de vos bras.

V/ Traduisez les phrases suivantes :

1/ I started running track when I was 10 years old.

2/ You must often make decisions in a split second when playing video games.

3/ Gymnastics requires a lot of strength and flexibility.

4/ Amélie qualified for the next Olympic Games.

5/ We have tennis practice at 9am every day.

BONUS : Quelques expressions idiomatiques :

1/ Jeter l'éponge : perdre espoir de réussir, renoncer à agir.

2/ Passer le flambeau : confier à d'autres la continuation d'une tâche.

3/ Attaquer la dernière ligne droite : être sur le point de terminer un projet. Expression qui vient des courses hippiques quand les chevaux doivent faire un dernier effort pour arriver à la victoire.

4/ Damer le pion à quelqu'un : prendre avantage ou l'emporter sur quelqu'un. Expression qui vient du jeu d'échecs ou de dames.

Réponses / Answer Key :

I	II	III	IV
1/ b	1/ b	1/ échouer, rater	1/ d
2/ a	2/ c	2/ démarrer, commencer	2/ c
3/ d	3/ a	3/ attraper, agripper	3/ a
4/ d	4/ d	4/ se relever, se redresser	4/ e
5/ a	5/ e	5/ poser, baisser	5/ b

V
1/ J'ai commencé à faire de l'athlétisme à l'âge de 10 ans (quand j'avais 10 ans.)
2/ Vous devez souvent prendre des décisions en une fraction de seconde (en quelque secondes) quand vous jouez à des jeux vidéo.
3/ La gymnastique requiert/exige beaucoup de force et de souplesse.
4/ Amélie s'est qualifiée pour les prochains Jeux Olympiques.
5/ Nous avons notre entrainement de tennis à 9 heures tous les matins.

CHAPITRE 17

Les pays, les nationalités & les voyages /

Countries, Nationalities & Travels

I/ Choisissez la bonne réponse :

1/ Dans ce groupe, il n'y a qu'un _____ allemand.
    a/ citoyenne
    b/ gens
    c/ personne
    d/ citoyen

2/ Quand je pars en voyage, j'aime partir à l'aventure et être
_____.
    a/ dépaysé
    b/ sans pays
    c/ du pays
    d/ paysan

3/ Ces trois directeurs de grandes sociétés internationales
partent en Inde pour un voyage ____ pour signer des contrats
importants.
    a/ d'agrément
    b/ d'affaires
    c/ de noces
    d/ de formation

4/ Cette station balnéaire est très populaire avec les jeunes en
période _____.
    a/ hivernale
    b/ estivale
    c/ pastorale
    d/ bicéphale

5/ Nous avons réservé _____ en Méditerranée.

    a/ une randonnée
    b/ une escalade
    c/ une croisière
    d/ une virée

II/ De quelle nationalité sont les personnes suivantes ? :

1/ Sophie (Belgique) : elle est _____.

2/ José (Mexique) : il est _____.

3/ Greta (Allemagne) : elle est _____.

4/ Meera et Kelly (France) : elles sont _____.

5/ Fatima (Indonésie) : elle est _____.

III/ Les pays suivants sont-ils masculins ou féminins ? :

1/ Italie : ___	6/ Chine : ____
2/ Argentine : ____	7/ Népal : ___
3/ Sénégal : ____	8/ Luxembourg : ____
4/ Liban : _____	9/ Hongrie : ____
5/ Japon : ____	10/ Afghanistan : ____

IV/ Associez les noms suivants à leur définition :

a/ une escale	b/ un séjour	c/ une location
d/ se renseigner		e/ attachez vos ceintures

1/ ___ : l'utilisation d'une voiture ou d'une propriété pour les vacances.

2/ ___ : vous le faites quand vous êtes perdu et voulez obtenir des indications.

3/ ___ : c'est un arrêt entre deux destinations.

4/ ___ : action de séjourner dans un endroit pendant un certain temps.

5/ ___ : c'est l'annonce que les passagers entendent avant le décollage ou l'atterrissage.

V/ Traduisez les phrases suivantes :

1/ We spent a month discovering all the regions of India.

2/ I cancelled my European trip two days ago.

3/ You should start packing for your trip tomorrow.

4/ Breakfast is served in the main dining-room.

5/ Don't forget to return your room key when checking out.

BONUS : Voici les surnoms de certains pays couramment utilisés en français :

1/ L'Hexagone : la France

2/ Le Rocher : Monaco

3/ Le plat pays : la Belgique

4/ L'Empire du milieu : la Chine

5/ Le Pays du soleil levant : le Japon

BONUS : Quelques expressions idiomatiques :

1/ Ce n'est pas le Pérou : une situation négative ou décevante.

2/ Être fort comme un Turc : être musclé, fort physiquement

3/ Parler [anglais, allemand, etc.] comme une vache espagnole : très mal parler une langue étrangère

4/ Filer à l'anglaise : s'éclipser/partir discrètement

5/ Bâtir des châteaux en Espagne : faire des projets impossibles.

Réponses / Answer Key :

I	II	III		IV
1/ d	1/ belge	1/ F	6/ F	1/ c
2/ a	2/ mexicain	2/ F	7/ M	2/ d
3/ b	3/ allemande	3/ M	8/ M	3/ a
4/ b	4/ françaises	4/ M	9/ F	4/ b
5/ c	5/ indonésienne	5/ M	10/ M	5/ e

V
1/ Nous avons passé un mois à découvrir toutes les régions de l'Inde.
2/ J'ai annulé notre voyage en Europe il y a deux jours.
3/ Vous devriez/Tu devrais commencer à faire ta valise/tes valises/tes bagages pour ton voyage demain.
4/ Le petit-déjeuner est servi dans la salle à manger principale.
5/ N'oublie pas/N'oubliez pas de rendre la clé de votre chambre quand vous quitterez l'hôtel.

CHAPITRE 18

Les achats / Shopping

I/ Choisissez la bonne réponse :

1/ Hier, j'ai fait_____ en achetant ces bottes pour 25 euros.
    a/ un marchandage
    b/ un marché
    c/ une occasion
    d/ une bonne affaire

2/ Je n'ai pas _____. Juste un billet de 50 euros.
    a/ d'argenterie
    b/ de liquide
    c/ de monnaie
    d/ de Monet

3/ _____ n'est pas incluse dans le prix d'achat de ce canapé.
    a/ Le déménagement
    b/ Le transport
    c/ La délivrance
    d/ La livraison

4/ N'oublie pas de _____ les outils pour les travaux de rénovation de la cuisine.
    a/ commander
    b/ ordonner
    c/ télécharger
    d/ prescrire

5/ Tu devrais essayer un autre modèle de pantalon. Celui-ci ne t'/te____ pas du tout.
    a/ aille
    b/ va
    c/ fait
    d/ t'accorde

II/ Éliminez l'intrus :

1/ des bottes/des sandales/des baskets/des gants/des mocassins

2/ gratuit/en promotion/cher/bon marché/en solde

3/ un sac/un cabas/un panier/un caddie/un tabouret

4/ une parfumerie/un supermarché/une supérette/une épicerie/ une grande surface

5/ faire des achats/faire des courses/faires des commissions/ faires des emplettes/faire des mots croisés

III/ Les Vêtements & les accessoires : complétez les phrases avec les mots proposés :

a/ des chaussettes	b/ des lunettes de soleil	c/ un chemisier
d/ un costume	e/ en survêtement	

1/ J'ai froid aux pieds. Je vais aller mettre _____.

2/ Marco a un entretien d'embauche demain. Il va mettre __.

3/ Il faut porter _____ quand on conduit en été.

4/ Les enfants font du sport _____ pendant leur cours de gym.

5/ Vous pouvez porter _____ pour aller à une soirée élégante.

IV/ Associez les artisans suivants avec les réparations qu'ils/elles peuvent effectuer ou les services qu'ils/elles peuvent proposer :

a/ un cordonnier	b/ un coiffeur	c/ un poissonnier
d/ une couturière	e/ une esthéticienne	

1/ _____ : elle vous fait un nettoyage de peau ou une épilation.

2/ _____ : il peut préparer un plateau de fruits de mer.

3/ _____ : il répare une paire de chaussures trouées.

4/ _____ : elle fait l'ourlet d'un pantalon trop long.

5/ _____ : il peut vous teindre les cheveux ou les couper.

V/ Dans quel commerce peut-on faire les achats suivants :

a/ un roman ou une bande-dessinée	b/ des croissants	c/ des médicaments
d/ un kilo de pommes ou une bouteille d'eau	e/ remplacer le bracelet d'une montre	

1/ _____ : une horlogerie/bijouterie

2/ _____ : une épicerie

3/ _____ : une librairie

4/ _____ : une boulangerie

5/ _____ : une pharmacie

BONUS : Quelques expressions idiomatiques :

1/ L'habit ne fait pas le moine : l'apparence peut être trompeuse.

2/ C'est un gros bonnet : c'est un personnage important.

3/ En avoir plein les bottes : être très fatigué après une longue marche ou un très gros effort.

4/ Rendre son tablier : démissionner.

5/ Retourner sa veste : changer complètement d'opinion.

6/ C'est fort de café (familier) ! : c'est exagéré !

BONUS : Quelques marques françaises célèbres:

1/ Les biscuits LU : société fondée en 1846. Slogan (tagline) du fameux Petit-Beurre LU : « qui me croque, craque, qui m'a croqué, recroquera ! »

2/ Les petits appareils ménagers MOULINEX : société fondée en 1937. Slogan : « Cuisiner devient facile »

3/ L'ORÉAL : société de cosmétiques créée en 1909. Le slogan actuel « Parce que nous le valons bien » a beaucoup évolué. Le slogan original date de 1971 pour une teinture de cheveux : « Ce n'est pas que je me soucie de l'argent. Ce qui compte le plus, c'est le bien-être de mes cheveux. En fait, peu importe que L'Oréal me fasse dépenser plus. C'est parce que je le vaux. ».

Réponses / Answer Key :

I	II	III	IV	V
1/ d	1/ des gants	1/ a	1/ e	1/ e
2/ c	2/ cher	2/ d	2/ c	2/ d
3/ d	3/ un tabouret	3/ b	3/ a	3/ a
4/ a	4/ une parfumerie	4/ e	4/ d	4/ b
5/ b	5/ faire des mots croisés	5/ c	5/ b	5/ c

CHAPITRE 19

Le monde du travail / The Workplace

I/ Choisissez la bonne réponse :

1/ Carla vient de perdre son emploi. Elle peut toucher des allocations _____ si elle s'inscrit la semaine prochaine.

    a/ familiales
    b/ logement
    c/ voyage
    d/ chômage

2/ N'oubliez pas de mettre votre _____ à jour avant votre entretien.

    a/ CV
    b/ CVS
    c/ VC
    d/ RV

3/ Cette semaine, mes _____ sont vendredi et samedi.

    a/ jours de paix
    b/ jours sans travail
    c/ journées
    d/ jours de repos

4/ Lucas vient d'avoir 62 ans. Il peut maintenant envisager de prendre _____.

    a/ son traitement
    b/ son départ
    c/ sa retraite
    d/ son retrait

5/ Les ouvriers vont travailler à _____ à 5 heures du matin.

a/ l'usine
b/ l'usure
c/ l'usufruit
d/ l'usurpateur

II/ Complétez les phrases avec les mots proposés :

a/ pénible	b/ démissionner	c/ une manifestation

d/ le comité d'entreprise	e/ faire grève

1/ Il est impossible de passer par les Champs-Elysées parce qu'il y a _____.

2/ C'est _____ qui a organisé notre voyage en Espagne au mois de juillet.

3/ Je pense que Jean-Marc va _____ parce qu'il n'aime pas l'ambiance de son bureau.

4/ Les ouvriers de cette usine se plaignent beaucoup car le travail est vraiment _____.

5/ Pour exprimer leur mécontentement dans cette entreprise, les ouvriers vont _____ à partir de lundi.

III/ Masculin ou féminin ? :

1/ emploi : __	6/ entretien : ___
2/ personnel : ___	7/ conseil d'administration : ___
3/ salaire : ___	8/ revendication : ___
4/ entreprise : ___	9/ banderole : ___
5/ croissance : ___	10/ offre : ___

IV/ Associez les noms suivants à leur définition :

a/ un fonctionnaire	b/ un syndicat	c/ une intérimaire

d/ licencier	e/ embaucher

1/ ___ : c'est une organisation qui défend les droits des travailleurs ou des employés.

2/ ___ : un patron y est souvent obligé quand un salarié fait une faute professionnelle.

3/ ___ : le gouvernement paie son salaire.

4/ ___ : c'est un synonyme d'engager ou de recruter.

5/ ___ : elle remplace une employée ou une ouvrière pour une durée très courte.

V/ Traduisez les phrases suivantes :

1/ Sarah recently got hired by the Disney company.

2/ More and more international companies will merge next year.

3/ The CEO of this car company is French.

4/ I have been working full-time for the past six months.

5/ The staff meeting is scheduled for 10am this morning.

BONUS : Quelques expressions idiomatiques :

1/ Renvoyer l'ascenseur à quelqu'un : rendre un service à quelqu'un qui vous a aidé dans le passé.

2/ Mettre les bouchées doubles : travailler beaucoup plus pour terminer un projet.

3/ Avoir du pain sur la planche : avoir beaucoup de travail.

4/ Ne pas attendre 107 ans : expression qui exprime la frustration de pas obtenir ce que l'on veut plus rapidement.

5/ Ça porte ses fruits : donner des résultats, être fructueux.

6/ C'est dans mes cordes : j'ai les capacités pour faire quelque chose. Expression d'origine musicale du 19ème siècle qui se disait d'un chanteur avec d'excellentes cordes vocales.

BONUS : *Citations Littéraires :*

1/ « L'emploi qu'un homme finit par obtenir est rarement celui pour lequel il se croyait préparé et dans lequel il pensait pouvoir être utile. » Marguerite Yourcenar, Romancière, Essayiste. Première femme à intégrer l'Académie française en 1980 (1903-1987).

2/ « Le plus beau métier d'homme est le métier d'unir les hommes. » Antoine de Saint-Exupéry, Artiste, Aviateur, Écrivain (1900-1944).

3/ « Il faut être enthousiaste de son métier pour y exceller. » Denis Diderot, Philosophe, Critique d'art (1713-1784).

4/ « Les conseils et les compliments sincères rendent le travail facile et doux. » Alexandre Dumas fils, Romancier, Dramaturge (1824-1895).

5/ « La racine du travail est parfois amère, mais la saveur de ses fruits est toujours exquise. » Victor Hugo, Artiste, Écrivain, Poète, Romancier, Homme politique (1802-1885).

Réponses / Answer Key :

I	II	III		IV
1/ d	1/ c	1/ M	6/ M	1/ b
2/ a	2/ d	2/ M	7/ M	2/ d
3/ d	3/ b	3/ M	8/ F	3/ a
4/ c	4/ a	4/ F	9/ F	4/ e
5/ a	5/ e	5/ F	10/ F	5/ c

V
1/ Sarah vient d'être embauchée/engagée par la société Disney.
2/ De plus en plus de sociétés internationales fusionneront l'année prochaine.
3/ Le PDG (président directeur général) de cette marque automobile est français.
4/ Je travaille à plein-temps depuis six mois.
5/ La réunion du personnel est programmée/prévue à 10 heures ce matin.

CHAPITRE 20

Le monde de la politique / Political Life

I/ Choisissez la bonne réponse :

1/ Ce candidat n'a pas réussi à obtenir assez de _____ pour se faire élire.

    a/ voies
    b/ voie
    c/ voix
    d/ voit

2/ Le président de la République envisage de se présenter pour un deuxième _____.

    a/ durée
    b/ période
    c/ mandat
    d/ terme

3/ En 2019, l'Assemblée Nationale comptait 577 _____.

    a/ représentants
    b/ députés
    c/ personnels
    d/ conseillers

4/ Pour voter, il faut mettre _____ dans l'urne.

    a/ le papier
    b/ la feuille
    c/ le bulletin
    d/ le vote

5/ Le Président va bientôt _____ son premier ministre.

    a/ appointer
    b/ déclarer
    c/ nominer
    d/ nommer

II/ Choisissez l'endroit où les personnes suivantes exercent leur profession :

a/ une reine	b/ un préfet	c/ une députée
d/ un conseiller municipal		e/ un sénateur

1/ ___ : une Préfecture

2/ ___ : l'Assemblée Nationale

3/ ___ : le Sénat

4/ ___ : une mairie

5/ ___ : un royaume

III/ Associez les noms suivants à leur définition :

a/ un dirigeant	b/ la porte-parole	c/ écologiste
d/ le maire		e/ une politique

1/ ___ : elle présente les décisions gouvernementales au public et à la presse.

2/ ___ : il dirige les affaires administratives d'un village ou d'une ville.

3/ ___ : ce sont des options/décisions prises par un gouvernement dans plusieurs domaines.

4/ ___ : c'est une personne qui commande une institution.

5/ ___ : il/elle intègre des mesures de protection de l'environnement dans son programme politique.

IV/ Transformez les noms suivants en adjectifs :

1/ un électeur : une campagne _____.

2/ le président : une délégation _____.

3/ le Parlement : un assistant _____.

4/ un ministère : une décision _____.

5/ une législation : des élections _____.

V/ Associez les acronymes des grandes institutions internationales à leur rôles :

a/ ONU (l'Organisation des Nations Unies)	b/ OMS (l'Organisation mondiale de la santé)	c/ OTAN (l'Organisation du traité de l'Atlantique Nord)
d/ FMI (le Fonds monétaire international)		e/ CPI (Cour pénale internationale)

1/ _____ : l'organisation qui garantit la stabilité financière mondiale.

2/ _____ : c'est une alliance politique et militaire.

3/ _____ : elle gère les crises sanitaires mondiales.

4/ _____ : elle est chargée de juger les cas de génocides, de crimes contre l'humanité et de guerre.

5/ _____ : son but est de maintenir la paix et la sécurité mondiale.

BONUS : Quelques expressions idiomatiques :

1/ Avoir le bras long : avoir beaucoup de contacts influents.

2/ Mettre des bâtons dans les roues : gêner le déroulement de quelque chose.

3/ Faire la pluie et le beau temps : se croire tout permis, décider de tout.

4/ Ne pas avoir la/sa langue dans sa poche : aimer beaucoup parler.

5/ Tâter le terrain : évaluer une situation avant de prendre une décision ou d'agir.

6/ Il y a anguille sous roche : on le dit pour décrire une situation bizarre ou qui n'est pas claire.

BONUS : Citations Littéraires :

1/ « La bonne politique est de faire croire aux peuples qu'ils sont libres. » Napoléon Bonaparte, Empereur, Général, Homme d'état, Militaire (1769-1821).

2/ « En littérature, je suis pour le grand contre le petit, et, en politique, je suis pour les petits contre les grands. » Victor Hugo, Artiste, Écrivain, Poète, Romancier, Homme politique (1802-1885).

3/ « Tout l'art du dialogue politique consiste à parler tout seul à tour de rôle. » & « Les Français raffolent des révolutions mais ils ont horreur du changement. » André Frossard, Journaliste, Essayiste, Académicien (1915-1995).

Réponses / Answer Key :

I	II	III	IV	V
1/ c	1/ b	1/ b	1/ électorale	1/ d
2/ c	2/ c	2/ d	2/ présidentielle	2/ c
3/ b	3/ e	3/ e	3/ parlementaire	3/ b
4/ c	4/ d	4/ a	4/ ministérielle	4/ e
5/ d	5/ a	5/ c	5/ législatives	5/ a

BONUS : Révision du vocabulaire

_____ / 25

I/ Choisissez la réponse correcte :

1/ Pour égoutter des légumes, on utilise _____.
    a/ une passoire
    b/ une mangeoire
    c/ un grimoire
    d/ un prétoire

2/ Dans ce groupe, il n'y a qu'un _____ allemand.
    a/ citoyenne
    b/ gens
    c/ personne
    d/ citoyen

3/ J'adore _____ de cette chanson. Elles sont très poétiques.
    a/ le langage
    b/ les mots
    c/ les paroles
    d/ la langue

4/ _____ sont des organes vitaux.
    a/ L'orteil/le cœur/les poumons
    b/ Le cœur/l'oreille/le cerveau
    c/ Le foie/le cœur/les reins
    d/ Le bras/le cerveau/le pancréas

5/ Après fait un jogging d'une heure, j'ai des _____.
    a/ courbatures
    b/ courgettes
    c/ conjonctures
    d/ vergetures

II/ Éliminez l'intrus :

1/ une cabane/un manoir/un château/une forteresse/un palais

2/ inquiet/soucieux/sur le qui-vive/rassuré/tourmenté

3/ un cachet/un sirop/une gélule/une pastille/une capsule

4/ un stagiaire/un apprenti/un musicien/un élève/un lycéen

5/ un sac/un cabas/un panier/un caddie/un tabouret

III/ Masculin ou féminin :

1/ olive : _____	6/ stationnement : _____
2/ peignoir : ___	7/ des pantoufles : _____
3/ saison : _____	8/ revendication : ___
4/ salaire : ___	9/ dispute : _____
5/ abonnement : _____	10/ équipage : _____

IV/ Associez les mots suivants à leur définition :

a/ un blouson	b/ un bagagiste	c/ un sondage
d/ tricher		e/ licencier

1/ ___ : un patron le fait souvent quand un salarié fait une faute professionnelle.

2/ ___ : c'est une pratique malhonnête dans n'importe quel jeu ou examen.

3/ ___ : il met vos valises dans la soute de l'avion.

4/ ___ : il tient chaud quand on fait de la moto.

5/ ___ : c'est une méthode statistique qui sonde l'opinion publique.

V/ *Traduisez les phrases suivantes :*

1/ The CEO of this car company is French.

2/ Gymnastics requires a lot of strength and flexibility.

3/ The concert was cancelled at the last minute.

4/ They like to wear linen clothes in the summer.

5/ Pedestrians must watch out when crossing the streets.

Réponses / Answer Key :

I	II	III		IV
1/ a	1/ une cabane	1/ F	6/ M	1/ e
2/ d	2/ rassuré	2/ M	7/ F	2/ d
3/ c	3/ un sirop	3/ F	8/ F	3/ b
4/ c	4/ un musicien	4/ M	9/ F	4/ a
5/ a	5/ un tabouret	5/ M	10/ M	5/ c

V
1/ Le PDG (président directeur général) de cette société d'automobile est français.
2/ La gymnastique exige/requiert beaucoup de force et de souplesse.
3/ Le concert a été annulé à la dernière minute.
4/ Ils aiment porter/mettre des vêtements en lin en été.
5/ Les piétons doivent faire attention avant de traverser la rue

ABOUT THE
AUTHOR

Born in Versailles and raised in Paris, Véronique graduated from Paris-III Sorbonne Nouvelle (B.A. in English/M.A. in American Studies) while working for an American Junior Year Abroad Program in Paris. She went on to teach French Culture and Cinema at Tufts University and Boston University for 15 years. She graduated from the School of Communications at Boston University (M.S. in Advertising & Public Relations).

Shortly after graduating from UCLA with a Certificate in Film Distribution & Marketing, she worked for several film distribution companies.

In 2004, she founded her own film distribution company, Casque d'or films. In 2008, she wrote and directed an animated short film that premiered at the AFI Film Festival in Los Angeles. In 2010, she wrote and directed an animated short series entitled THE QUEER PET ADVENTURES. Both titles screened at many film festivals worldwide and are currently distributed in French and German territories.

Since settling in Los Angeles, she has also worked as a French Instructor at the Beverly Hills Lingual Institute and has taught language seminars at the Alliance Française of Los Angeles.

Her first published novel, written in French, is entitled, The Parisian Adventures of Kimberly. It is a French Reader, a novel intended to help intermediate learners of French to review the language in an entertaining and relaxed way. The book is part of a three-book set, composed of the novel written in French, the Activity Book that includes a wide variety of French vocabulary practice exercises, and the Answer key that provides answers to all the exercises.

Véronique just completed her second French Reader entitled *Treasure in Occitania*. She is also working on two other novels and two English to French Translation Workbooks for intermediate and advanced learners of French. Besides writing, she is currently training as a baker and pastry chef.

CONNECT WITH

Véronique F. Courtois

Twitter:
@vfcfrenchauthor

LinkedIn
www.linkedin.com/in/veronique-courtois-72486616

DEAR READER...

Thank you for purchasing my books! I hope you're enjoying or enjoyed reading them.

As a bilingual writer, I always seek to write stories that will interest my readers and allow them to become more familiar with the French language and culture. So I would mostly welcome your suggestions and I'd be very grateful for the lovely comments! I'd be delighted if you could leave an honest review on Amazon as well. I love reading reviews for my books.

To leave a review, your can either search *The Ultimate French Quiz Book for Beginner & Intermediate Levels* by Véronique F. Courtois on Amazon, click the book and leave a review

Or you could email me at **vfcfrenchbooks@gmail.com**. I welcome all suggestions and comments.

Thank you again for your interest. Keep learning French!

OTHER BOOKS BY

Véronique F. Courtois

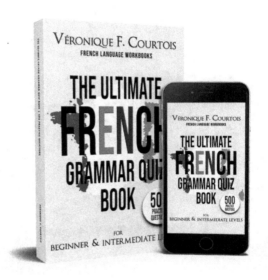

The Ultimate French Quiz Book for Beginner & Intermediate Levels: 500 Grammar Practice Questions (French Language Workbooks)

Refresh your French grammar skills with 500 multiple-choice questions on all the main grammar topics*. The book is divided into twenty short chapters. An evaluation test, a final diagnostic test, and answer keys are included. A perfect French review for all students of French!

Check it out on Amazon:
www.amazon.com/gp/product/0998080462

The Parisian Adventures of Kimberly
(Les Aventures Parisiennes de Kimberly):
A Franco-American Love Story

A perfect French for students book! This story has been made easier to understand by dividing each of the chapters into three parts. Key vocabulary has been highlighted, and the corresponding translations can be found in a box right beneath each section. This will provide you, the reader, with immediate support, and will help to ensure a great learning experience.

Activity Book for
The Parisian Adventures of Kimberly

This French reader workbook has been written to complement the intermediate level French reader novel entitled The Parisian Adventures of Kimberly by Véronique F. Courtois. This book fulfills a double purpose: Practicing reading comprehension and review vocabulary through a large variety of French reading exercises.

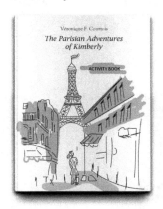

Answer Key to the Activity Book for
The Parisian Adventures of Kimberly

This Answer Key book provides Intermediate French learners with the answers to reading comprehension questions, translation exercises and a wide variety of vocabulary exercises included in the Activity Book for The Parisian Adventures of Kimberly: Intermediate Level French Reader that supports B1, B2, and C1 levels of French proficiency.

Check out the series on Amazon:
www.amazon.com/gp/product/B084M74WD5

A Guide to Embracing, Controlling, Mastering and Exceling with Your Emotions

John L. Fisher

Table of Contents

Mind Over Mood

Mind Over Mood

Mind Over Mood

Introduction

Lois had always been a bundle of emotions, struggling to keep them in check and often feeling overwhelmed by their intensity. Whether it was joy, sadness, anger, or fear, her emotions had a way of taking over her life. She yearned for stability and control, desperately wanting to find a way to master her feelings.

One day, while scrolling through an online bookstore, Lois stumbled upon a book that caught her attention. Its title, "Mind Over Mood," seemed to speak directly to her soul. Intrigued, she wasted no time in ordering it, hoping that it held the answers she had been seeking for so long.

When the book arrived, Lois eagerly opened it and began reading. Each page seemed to unveil a new revelation, like a guidebook to understanding and taming her emotions.

It taught her that it was okay to feel, to experience the full spectrum of emotions that life had to offer.

Mind Over Mood

The key, it said, was not to let those emotions dictate her actions and decisions.

As Lois delved deeper into the book, she realized that the true power lay in accepting her feelings rather than suppressing or denying them. She learned that emotions were a natural part of being human, and by acknowledging them, she could better understand herself and others. The book encouraged her to be compassionate towards herself and to embrace vulnerability as a strength, not a weakness.

Armed with this newfound knowledge, Lois started practicing mindfulness. She learned to observe her emotions without judgment, allowing them to rise and fall like waves without getting swept away. She discovered the importance of self-care, nurturing herself with activities that brought her joy and peace. She also began to open up to trusted friends and family, sharing her struggles and seeking support when needed.

With time, Lois noticed a transformation taking place within her. She became more self-aware, recognizing her triggers and understanding the underlying reasons behind her emotional reactions. She decided to react with empathy and tolerance rather than letting her anger rule her. When sadness engulfed her, she allowed herself to grieve, knowing that it was a temporary state that would eventually pass.

As Lois continued to apply the lessons from the book, she discovered a newfound sense of empowerment. She realized that mastering her emotions didn't mean suppressing them but rather harnessing their energy and redirecting it towards positive change. She became an advocate for her own well-being, setting boundaries and making choices that aligned with her values and aspirations.

Over time, Lois's relationships deepened and flourished. Her loved ones noticed the remarkable shift in her, and she became a source of inspiration

Mind Over Mood

for those around her. She shared her journey, recommending the book that had transformed her life, hoping to touch others in the same way it had touched her.

Lois's story serves as a testament to the power of self-reflection and personal growth. Through accepting her feelings and mastering her emotions, she not only transformed her own life but also became a beacon of light for others on their own journeys of self-discovery and emotional mastery.

In a world that often pushes us to suppress our emotions, "Mind Over Mood" serves as a guiding light through the labyrinth of our inner landscape. This transformative journey delves deep into the uncharted territories of our hearts, inviting us to embrace the full spectrum of our feelings and unlock the power within.

Prepare to embark on a captivating exploration that will reshape your understanding of emotions, ignite your personal growth, and ultimately lead you to the extraordinary art of emotional mastery. Get ready to unleash the untamed force of your emotions and embrace the liberation that awaits within these pages. The time has come to embark on a remarkable quest of self-discovery, where acceptance and mastery converge in perfect harmony.

Mind Over Mood

Chapter 1

Understanding Emotions

The Nature of Emotions

Emotions are an inherent part of the human experience, influencing our thoughts, behaviors, and overall well-being. Understanding the nature of emotions is crucial to accepting and mastering them. Emotions can be described as complex psychological and physiological responses to stimuli, both internal and external. They serve as valuable signals that provide insight into our needs, desires, and experiences.

Emotions encompass a wide range of feelings, including joy, sadness, anger, fear, love, surprise, and disgust. Each emotion carries its own unique characteristics and can vary in intensity and duration. It's important to recognize that emotions are neither good nor bad; they simply exist as part of our human nature.

Mind Over Mood

The Role of Emotions in Life

Emotions play a vital role in our lives, influencing various aspects of our decision-making processes, relationships, and overall well-being. They provide us with valuable information about ourselves and the world around us. Understanding and interpreting our emotions allows us to navigate through life with greater clarity and self-awareness.

Emotions serve several essential functions:

a) Communication: Emotions act as a form of communication, allowing us to express our internal states and connect with others on an emotional level. Facial expressions, body language, and tone of voice all convey emotions and help us understand the emotions of others.

b) Motivation: Emotions serve as powerful motivators that drive our actions and behaviors. For example, the fear of failure can motivate us to work harder, while the joy of success can reinforce our efforts and encourage us to continue pursuing our goals.

c) Decision-Making: Emotions provide valuable information that influences our decision-making processes. They serve as intuitive guides, helping us evaluate situations, weigh options, and make choices that align with our values and desires.

d) Self-Preservation: Certain emotions, such as fear, play a crucial role in our survival by alerting us to potential threats and danger. They trigger the "fight-or-flight" response, preparing our bodies to respond quickly and effectively in challenging situations.

Common Misconceptions about Emotions

Despite the significance of emotions in our lives, there are several misconceptions and misunderstandings that can hinder our ability to accept and master them effectively. It's important to address these misconceptions to develop a healthier relationship with our emotions:

Mind Over Mood

a) Emotions are Weakness: Some individuals perceive emotions as a sign of weakness or vulnerability. However, emotions are a fundamental aspect of being human, and acknowledging them requires strength and courage. Emotions provide valuable insights into our inner world and can guide us towards personal growth and self-discovery.

b) Emotions Should Be Suppressed: Society often encourages the suppression or avoidance of certain emotions, particularly those considered negative or uncomfortable, such as sadness or anger. However, suppressing emotions can lead to internal conflicts, increased stress, and even physical health issues. Accepting and understanding our emotions allows us to process them in a healthy and constructive manner.

c) Emotions Are Irrational: Emotions are sometimes dismissed as irrational or illogical, contrasting them with rational thinking. However, emotions serve an essential purpose and are not inherently irrational.

Mind Over Mood

They provide valuable information that complements our cognitive processes and helps us make well-rounded decisions.

d) Emotional Mastery Means Eliminating Negative Emotions: Mastering emotions does not imply the elimination of negative emotions entirely. Instead, it involves developing emotional intelligence, self-regulation, and coping strategies to navigate and channel these emotions effectively. The goal is to understand and accept the full spectrum of emotions while responding to them in a balanced and constructive way.

By understanding the nature of emotions, recognizing their role in our lives, and dispelling common misconceptions, we lay the foundation for accepting and mastering.

Part I:

Accepting

Your Feelings

Chapter 2

Emotional Awareness

Self-awareness is a fundamental aspect of emotional awareness. It involves being conscious of our thoughts, feelings, and behaviors in the present moment. Developing self-awareness allows us to observe and understand our emotions more accurately, enabling us to respond to them in a healthier and more constructive manner.

To cultivate self-awareness:

a) Mindfulness: Practicing mindfulness involves intentionally focusing our attention on the present moment without judgment. By engaging in mindfulness exercises such as meditation or deep breathing, we can cultivate a heightened sense of self-awareness and observe our emotions as they arise, without becoming overwhelmed or reactive.

b) Reflection: Taking time for self-reflection is essential for developing self-awareness. By setting

Mind Over Mood

aside moments of quiet contemplation, journaling, or engaging in introspective activities, we create space to explore our inner thoughts, feelings, and experiences. Reflecting on past events and emotional reactions can provide valuable insights into our patterns and triggers.

c) **Seeking Feedback:** Feedback from trusted friends, family members, or professionals can offer valuable external perspectives on our emotions and behaviors. Others may provide insights that we might not have considered, helping us gain a deeper understanding of ourselves.

Developing Self-Awareness

Recognizing and labeling our emotions accurately is crucial for emotional awareness. It allows us to understand the specific emotions we are experiencing, their triggers, and their impact on our thoughts and behaviors.

To improve our ability to recognize different emotions:

a) Emotional Vocabulary: Expanding our emotional vocabulary can enhance our ability to identify and articulate our feelings. By familiarizing ourselves with a broader range of emotion words, we become more adept at recognizing and expressing the nuances of our emotional experiences.

b) Body Sensations: Emotions are not solely experienced in our minds; they also manifest as physical sensations in our bodies. Paying attention to bodily cues, such as increased heart rate, muscle tension, or changes in breathing patterns, can provide valuable information about our emotional state.

c) Non-Verbal Cues: Emotions are often communicated through non-verbal cues, such as facial expressions, body language, and tone of voice. Being attentive to these cues, both in ourselves and in others, can deepen our understanding of the emotions present in a given situation.

Mind Over Mood

Recognizing Different Emotions

The ability to recognize different emotions can be an invaluable life skill. Whether we want to admit it or not, our emotions shape our lives in ways that we often cannot comprehend. Recognizing different emotions can help us identify our own feelings and the feelings of those around us, enabling us to make more informed decisions and communicate effectively.

One way to begin to recognize different emotions is to take a step back and start observing both our own and others' reactions. Not only is it important to observe body language and facial expressions, but it's also helpful to take a moment to think about why the other person might be feeling the way they are. We've all had times where we felt something deeply but couldn't quite put our finger on it, so recognizing our own feelings can be challenging. Once we understand our own emotions, we can begin to pay more attention to the feelings of those around us.

Mind Over Mood

Another way to hone your emotional recognition skills is by taking some time out of your day to reflect. This can help you keep track of how your own emotions are changing throughout the day. This reflection can also provide insight into how your emotions affect your actions, relationships, and experiences. Similarly, reflecting on the emotions of people around you can help you better understand what they're going through and how to support them.

Developing the ability to recognize different emotions can take a lot of time and practice, but it's well worth the effort. People who are able to recognize different emotions have a heightened capacity to understand themselves and the people around them. This skill provides valuable insight and can help us build more positive relationships.

The Importance of Emotional Intelligence

Emotional intelligence refers to the ability to recognize, understand, and manage our emotions effectively, as well as to recognize and empathize with the emotions of others. It encompasses several key components:

a) **Self-Awareness:** As discussed earlier, self-awareness forms the foundation of emotional intelligence. By being aware of our own emotions, we can better understand how they impact our thoughts, behaviors, and interactions with others.

b) **Self-Regulation:** Emotional intelligence involves developing the ability to regulate and manage our emotions appropriately. This includes strategies such as deep breathing exercises, practicing patience, and reframing negative thoughts.

c) Empathy: Empathy is the capacity to understand and share the feelings of others. By cultivating empathy, we can develop more meaningful and supportive relationships, as well as respond to others' emotions with compassion and understanding.

d) Social Skills: Emotional intelligence also encompasses effective communication, active listening, conflict resolution, and collaboration. Developing strong social skills allows us to navigate social situations with empathy and respect.

We can increase our emotional awareness, relationships, and general wellbeing by cultivating emotional intelligence. It enables us to navigate the complexities of our own emotions and understand the emotions of others, fostering healthier and more fulfilling connections with ourselves and those around us.

WISDOM

P
O
W
E
R

VISION

EMOTION

Mind Over Mood

Chapter 3

Exploring Uncomfortable Emotions

Dealing with Fear and Anxiety

Fear and anxiety are common and natural human emotions that can often feel overwhelming. Understanding how to deal with these emotions is essential for emotional well-being and personal growth.

a) Recognizing Fear and Anxiety: Fear is a response to a specific threat or danger, while anxiety is a more generalized sense of unease or worry. Identifying the specific triggers and manifestations of fear and anxiety in our lives can help us address them more effectively.

b) Mindfulness and Acceptance: Mindfulness practices, such as deep breathing and meditation, can help us develop a non-judgmental awareness of our fear and anxiety. By acknowledging these emotions without resistance, we can reduce their intensity and learn to respond to them with compassion.

c) Cognitive Restructuring: Fear and anxiety often arise from negative or irrational thought patterns. These ideas are recognized, contested, and replaced with more realistic and uplifting ones through cognitive restructuring. This process can help alleviate fear and anxiety by reframing our perception of the situation.

d) Gradual Exposure: If fear or anxiety is related to specific situations or objects, gradual exposure can be an effective approach. By gradually and systematically exposing ourselves to the feared stimulus in a safe and controlled manner, we can desensitize ourselves and reduce our emotional response over time.

Understanding and Managing Anger

Anger is a powerful emotion that, when not managed effectively, can lead to detrimental consequences for ourselves and those around us. Learning to understand and manage anger is crucial for maintaining healthy relationships and emotional well-being.

a) Anger Awareness: Recognizing the signs and triggers of anger is the first step in managing it effectively. Physical cues such as increased heart rate or tension in the body, as well as emotional signs like irritability or frustration, can indicate the presence of anger.

b) Anger Expression: Expressing anger in a healthy and constructive manner is essential. This involves finding appropriate outlets for anger, such as engaging in physical activity, journaling, or expressing oneself assertively rather than aggressively.

c) Anger Coping Strategies: Developing coping strategies can help manage anger in challenging situations. These strategies may include deep breathing exercises, taking a time-out to cool down, or using relaxation techniques to calm the body and mind.

d) Conflict Resolution: Learning effective conflict resolution skills can prevent anger from escalating into harmful or destructive behaviors. Techniques such as active listening, empathy, and assertive communication can facilitate constructive discussions and foster understanding between individuals.

Coping with Sadness and Grief

Sadness and grief are natural emotional responses to loss, change, or significant life events. Coping with these emotions in a healthy way is essential for emotional healing and moving forward.

a) Allowing Yourself to Feel: It's important to give yourself permission to experience and express sadness and grief. Allowing these emotions to surface without judgment or suppression is a crucial step in the healing process.

b) Self-Care and Support: Engaging in self-care activities, such as getting enough rest, maintaining a healthy diet, and seeking social support, can help alleviate the intensity of sadness and grief.

Connecting with loved ones, joining support groups, or seeking professional help can provide valuable emotional support during challenging times.

c) Rituals and Ceremonies: Rituals and ceremonies can provide structure and meaning to the grieving process. Engaging in activities such as creating a memory box, writing letters, or participating in memorial services can offer comfort and facilitate emotional healing.

d) Time for Reflection and Acceptance: When coping with loss and grief, it's important to allow oneself time for reflection and acceptance. Embracing the process of grieving, acknowledging the pain, and gradually accepting the loss can lead to healing and eventual emotional growth.

Mind Over Mood

Addressing Shame and Guilt

Shame and guilt are powerful and often uncomfortable emotions that can significantly impact our well-being and self-esteem. Learning to address and overcome shame and guilt is crucial for personal growth and emotional well-being.

a) Recognizing Shame and Guilt: Understanding the differences between shame and guilt is important. Shame is a deep-seated feeling of worthlessness or inadequacy, while guilt is the recognition of having done something wrong or violated our own values.

b) Challenging Shame-Based Beliefs: Shame is often rooted in negative self-perceptions and beliefs. Challenging these beliefs and replacing them with more compassionate and realistic thoughts can help alleviate shame and cultivate self-acceptance.

c) Making Amends and Learning from Guilt: Guilt can be an opportunity for growth and learning. Acknowledging the actions or behaviors that led to

Mind Over Mood

guilt, taking responsibility, and making amends where appropriate can facilitate healing and growth.

d) Practicing Self-Compassion: Developing self-compassion is crucial when addressing shame and guilt. Treating ourselves with kindness, understanding that we are human and make mistakes, and practicing self-forgiveness can help release the burden of shame and guilt.

Managing Jealousy and Envy

Jealousy and envy are complex emotions that can arise when we perceive a threat to our sense of security, self-worth, or possessions. Learning to manage jealousy and envy is essential for maintaining healthy relationships and personal well-being.

a) Understanding the Underlying Triggers: Identifying the underlying causes and triggers of jealousy and envy is crucial. This may involve exploring feelings of insecurity, comparison, or unmet needs that contribute to these emotions.

b) Cultivating Gratitude: Practicing gratitude can counteract feelings of jealousy and envy by shifting our focus to appreciating what we have rather than what others possess. Regularly acknowledging and expressing gratitude for our blessings can help cultivate contentment and reduce feelings of envy.

c) Building Self-Confidence: Developing self-confidence and a strong sense of self-worth is key to managing jealousy and envy. Engaging in activities that foster personal growth, pursuing passions and interests, and celebrating personal achievements can boost self-esteem and reduce the need for comparison.

d) Open Communication and Trust: In relationships, jealousy and envy can strain trust and create conflict. Open communication, honesty, and expressing vulnerabilities can help address these emotions within the context of relationships. Building trust and fostering a supportive and secure environment can help manage jealousy and envy effectively.

Chapter 4

Cultivating Self-Compassion

Self-compassion involves treating oneself with kindness, understanding, and care, especially during challenging times. By developing a compassionate relationship with ourselves, we can navigate our emotions with greater ease, build resilience, and foster emotional well-being. This chapter explores various strategies and practices to help you cultivate self-compassion and embrace a positive self-image.

Practicing Kindness and Understanding

The journey towards self-compassion begins with practicing kindness and understanding towards ourselves. Often, we are quick to criticize and judge ourselves harshly when we experience difficult emotions or make mistakes. However, by adopting a kind and understanding attitude, we can counteract self-judgment and cultivate a more compassionate perspective. This section explores techniques such as self-talk reframing, self-encouragement, and treating ourselves as we would a close friend or loved one.

Letting Go of Self-Judgment

Self-judgment is a common barrier to self-compassion. It involves harshly evaluating ourselves based on perceived flaws, mistakes, or shortcomings. In this section, we explore methods for letting go of self-judgment, such as challenging negative self-talk, practicing self-forgiveness, and embracing self-acceptance. By recognizing that we are imperfect beings, just like everyone else, we can free ourselves from the burden of self-judgment and create space for self-compassion to flourish.

Embracing Imperfections

Embracing imperfections is an essential aspect of self-compassion. We all have strengths and weaknesses, successes and failures, and accepting this reality allows us to develop a healthier relationship with ourselves. This section delves into the concept of embracing imperfections, encouraging self-growth, and shifting the focus from self-criticism to self-improvement. By embracing our flaws as opportunities for growth and learning, we can foster self-compassion and develop a more positive self-image.

Nurturing a Positive Self-Image

A positive self-image is crucial for cultivating self-compassion. When we view ourselves in a positive light, it becomes easier to treat ourselves with kindness, respect, and compassion. This section explores strategies for nurturing a positive self-image, including self-affirmations, practicing gratitude for our strengths and accomplishments, and developing a healthy sense of self-worth.

By consciously focusing on our positive qualities and achievements, we can enhance our self-compassion and build a solid foundation for emotional well-being.

You will gradually increase your capacity for self-compassion by implementing the techniques and methods described in this chapter.

On the road to accepting your feelings and controlling your emotions, it's crucial to embrace kindness, let go of self-judgment, embrace faults, and cultivate a positive self-image.

Remember that practicing self-compassion is treating oneself with the same respect and understanding that you would extend to others, rather than engaging in self-indulgence or avoiding responsibility. You can develop emotional resilience, deal with difficulties more easily, and live a more satisfying and well-balanced life by practicing self-compassion.

Part II:

Mastering Your

Emotions

Chapter 5

Emotion Regulation Strategies

Emotions are a natural part of being human, but it's crucial to learn how to effectively manage and regulate them. By understanding the triggers, patterns, and processes behind our emotions, we can develop skills and techniques to regulate them in a healthy and constructive manner. This chapter explores various strategies and techniques that can help individuals gain better control over their emotions and achieve emotional balance in their lives.

Identifying Triggers and Patterns

The first step in emotion regulation is to identify the triggers and patterns that lead to specific emotional responses. Emotions can be triggered by external factors such as certain situations, events, or interactions, as well as internal factors like thoughts, beliefs, and memories. By becoming more aware of these triggers and patterns, individuals can gain insights into their emotional reactions and take proactive steps to manage them.

Deep Breathing and Relaxation Techniques

Deep breathing and relaxation techniques are powerful tools for regulating emotions. When we experience intense emotions, our breathing tends to become shallow and rapid, exacerbating the emotional response. By consciously focusing on our breath and engaging in deep, slow breaths, we can activate the body's relaxation response and calm our emotions. Additionally, incorporating relaxation techniques such as progressive muscle relaxation or guided imagery can further enhance the relaxation response and promote emotional balance.

Cognitive Restructuring for Emotional Balance

Cognitive restructuring involves challenging and modifying the negative or irrational thoughts that contribute to intense emotional reactions. Our thoughts play a significant role in shaping our emotional experiences, and by examining and reframing these thoughts, we can regulate our emotions more effectively. This process involves identifying and questioning distorted thinking patterns, replacing them with more balanced and realistic thoughts, and developing a more constructive and positive mindset.

Practicing Mindfulness in Daily Life

Mindfulness is a practice that cultivates present-moment awareness and non-judgmental acceptance of our thoughts, feelings, and sensations. By practicing mindfulness, individuals can develop the ability to observe their emotions without immediately reacting to them.

This allows for a greater sense of control and the opportunity to choose how to respond to emotions, rather than being driven by impulsive reactions. Mindfulness practices such as mindful breathing, body scan meditation, and mindful movement can be incorporated into daily life to promote emotional regulation.

By incorporating these emotion regulation strategies into one's life, individuals can gain greater mastery over their emotions and achieve emotional balance. It's important to note that mastering emotion regulation is an ongoing process that requires patience, practice, and self-compassion. Regularly engaging in these strategies can lead to increased emotional resilience, improved interpersonal relationships, and enhanced overall well-being.

Furthermore, it is essential to remember that seeking professional help or guidance from a therapist or counselor can be highly beneficial when navigating complex emotional challenges. A trained professional can provide personalized support, teach additional coping techniques, and assist in developing a tailored approach to emotion regulation that aligns with an individual's unique needs and circumstances.

Mind Over Mood

Chapter 6

Building Resilience

Resilience refers to the ability to adapt and bounce back from adversity, challenges, and setbacks. It is a crucial skill in mastering emotions and leading a fulfilling life. Building resilience allows individuals to navigate through difficult situations, maintain emotional well-being, and continue pursuing their goals and aspirations. This chapter focuses on developing resilience as a foundation for mastering emotions.

Developing Emotional Resilience

Emotional resilience involves cultivating inner strength and coping mechanisms to effectively deal with life's ups and downs. This section explores various strategies to enhance emotional resilience:

1. Building Self-Awareness: Developing an understanding of one's emotions, triggers, and

Mind Over Mood

patterns is fundamental in building resilience. By recognizing how emotions influence thoughts and behaviors, individuals can proactively manage their responses and make conscious choices.

2. Cultivating Positive Mindsets: Adopting a growth mindset and reframing challenges as opportunities for growth promotes resilience. Embracing optimism and focusing on solutions rather than dwelling on problems can significantly improve emotional resilience.

3. Practicing Self-Compassion: Self-compassion involves treating oneself with kindness, understanding, and acceptance. It entails recognizing and validating one's emotions while offering oneself support and care during difficult times. Self-compassion helps individuals bounce back from setbacks and promotes emotional well-being.

4. Developing Coping Strategies: Resilient individuals possess effective coping mechanisms to manage stress and adversity. This may include problem-solving skills, seeking social support, engaging in relaxation techniques, or engaging in hobbies and activities that promote emotional well-being.

Strengthening Mental Toughness

Mental toughness refers to the ability to remain focused, determined, and resilient in the face of challenges. It involves developing a resilient mindset and cultivating specific traits and skills:

1. Building Emotional Regulation Skills: Being able to regulate and manage emotions is crucial for mental toughness. This involves recognizing and acknowledging emotions without allowing them to overwhelm or control one's actions. Techniques like deep breathing, mindfulness, and cognitive restructuring can aid in emotional regulation.

2. Developing Perseverance: Resilient individuals demonstrate a high level of perseverance and determination. They persist in the face of obstacles, setbacks, and failures.

Mind Over Mood

44

Developing a growth mindset and setting achievable goals can foster perseverance and increase mental toughness.

3. Cultivating Self-Belief: Believing in oneself and one's abilities is a significant aspect of mental toughness. Developing self-confidence and a positive self-image helps individuals navigate challenges with resilience. Positive affirmations, visualization exercises, and celebrating personal achievements contribute to building self-belief.

4. Building Adaptability: Mental toughness involves being adaptable and flexible in the face of change and uncertainty. Resilient individuals can adjust their goals and strategies when necessary, embrace new circumstances, and find opportunities within challenges.

Enhancing Adaptive Coping Mechanisms

Adaptive coping mechanisms are strategies that promote psychological well-being and effective problem-solving. This section explores various techniques for enhancing adaptive coping mechanisms:

1. Seeking Social Support: Building a network of supportive relationships is essential for resilience. Having trusted individuals to lean on during difficult times provides emotional validation, guidance, and practical assistance. Connecting with others who share similar experiences can also provide a sense of belonging and validation.

2. Developing Problem-Solving Skills: Effective problem-solving involves breaking challenges into manageable steps, brainstorming solutions, and implementing them systematically. Developing problem-solving skills helps individuals feel empowered, reduces stress, and promotes resilience.

3. Practicing Stress Management: Managing stress is crucial for maintaining emotional well-being and building resilience. Techniques such as exercise, mindfulness, relaxation exercises, and time management can help individuals effectively cope with stressors.

4. Embracing a Healthy Lifestyle: A balanced lifestyle that includes proper nutrition, regular exercise, adequate sleep, and self-care activities contributes to overall emotional well-being and resilience. Taking care of physical health supports mental and emotional resilience.

Embracing Change and Uncertainty

The future can be unpredictable and uncertain—but with the right attitude, embracing change and uncertainty can be a useful practice for personal growth and development.

No one likes uncertainty, and it can be especially stressful when major changes impact your life. But with the right mindset, you can use change as an opportunity to evolve and grow. It's the same mentality that helps some of the most successful people handle difficult times and come out stronger in the end.

Mind Over Mood

First, recognize that this particular change involves growth. Even though it can be tough to move through the uncertainty, just remember that the discomfort will eventually lead to something positive. This is especially helpful when you don't know exactly where the future is headed.

Second, reach out for help or support when you need it. Talking to friends, family, or a professional can help you work through your feelings and come up with a plan for the days ahead.

Third, practice self-care. Taking time to do activities or hobbies that you enjoy can help improve your overall outlook, even if things feel chaotic. Exercise, meditation, and journaling are all great outlets for releasing stress.

Finally, focus on what you can control and find meaning in the present. Even if the future feels unpredictable, you can control how you feel in the moment. Concentrate on activities or things in life that bring you joy and try to make the most out of the current situation.

Mind Over Mood

Change and uncertainty is unavoidable, but how you approach it makes all the difference. With a positive attitude, you can use embracing change and uncertainty as an opportunity to evolve and move forward.

Chapter 7

Effective Communication

Effective communication is a fundamental aspect of mastering your emotions and fostering healthy relationships. It involves expressing your thoughts, feelings, and needs in a clear and assertive manner while also actively listening to others and empathizing with their perspectives. In this chapter, we will delve into the key components of effective communication and explore various strategies for improving your communication skills.

Assertive Communication Skills

Assertive communication is a style of communication that promotes honesty, respect, and open dialogue. It involves expressing your thoughts, feelings, and desires while considering the rights and needs of others. Here are some essential components of assertive communication:

Mind Over Mood

- Clear and Direct Expression: Assertive communicators express their thoughts and feelings clearly, avoiding ambiguity and passive-aggressive behavior. They avoid placing blame on others by using "I" expressions to accept responsibility for their feelings. By clearly stating their needs and expectations, they create a foundation for understanding and collaboration.

- Active Listening: Listening is a vital aspect of effective communication. Being an active listener means fully focusing on the speaker, giving them your undivided attention, and demonstrating empathy. Maintaining eye contact, showing attention by nodding or using other nonverbal signs, and asking follow-up questions to check knowledge are all part of it.

- Respectful Boundaries: Assertive communicators respect both their own boundaries and those of others. They recognize that each individual has the right to their own thoughts, opinions, and feelings.

They set boundaries by clearly communicating what is acceptable to them and actively listening to others' boundaries as well.

- Conflict Resolution: Assertive communication helps in resolving conflicts by fostering open dialogue and finding mutually satisfactory solutions. Assertive communicators approach conflicts with a problem-solving mindset, seeking to understand the perspectives of all parties involved and finding compromises that meet everyone's needs.

Active Listening and Empathy

Active listening goes beyond hearing words; it involves understanding the speaker's emotions, concerns, and underlying messages. When you practice active listening, you create a safe and supportive space for effective communication. Here are some strategies to enhance your active listening skills:

- Pay Attention: Ignore any outside noise and give the speaker your undivided attention.

Maintain eye contact, face the speaker, and use open and receptive body language to show your engagement.

- Reflective Listening: Reflect back what you've heard to ensure accurate understanding. Paraphrase or summarize the speaker's key points and feelings to demonstrate that you are actively listening and trying to comprehend their perspective.

- Show Empathy: This is the ability to comprehend and experience another person's feelings. Show empathy by putting yourself in the speaker's shoes, acknowledging their emotions, and validating their experiences. Expressing empathy helps create a connection and fosters a sense of understanding.

- Ask Open-Ended Questions: By posing open-ended questions, you can nudge the speaker to go into greater detail about their ideas and emotions. These questions prompt a more detailed response and allow for deeper exploration of the topic. Avoid asking leading or judgmental questions that may hinder open communication.

Conflict Resolution Strategies

Conflicts are a natural part of relationships, and learning effective conflict resolution strategies can help navigate these challenges constructively. Here are some key strategies for resolving conflicts:

- **Active Listening:** Actively listen to the perspectives of all parties involved in the conflict. Give each person an opportunity to express their feelings and concerns without interruption. This creates an atmosphere of mutual respect and understanding.

- **Seek Common Ground:** Look for areas of agreement or shared interests between the conflicting parties. Identifying common ground helps to build a foundation for finding solutions that meet everyone's needs.

- **Collaborative Problem Solving:** Engage in collaborative problem solving by brainstorming

Mind Over Mood

potential solutions together. Encourage creativity and open-mindedness while exploring various options. Try to discover solutions that benefit all parties involved and satisfy their requirements.

- **Use "I" Statements:** When expressing your concerns or frustrations, use "I" statements to take ownership of your feelings. For example, instead of saying, "You never listen to me," say, "I feel unheard when I don't feel listened to." This approach minimizes defensiveness and encourages open dialogue.

Building Healthy Relationships

Effective communication is the cornerstone of healthy relationships. By implementing the strategies mentioned earlier, you can foster healthier connections with others. Here are some additional tips for building and maintaining healthy relationships:

- **Trust and Honesty:** Build trust by being honest and reliable in your interactions. Trust forms the foundation for open communication and deeper connections.

- **Empathy and Understanding:** Cultivate empathy and understanding for others by considering their perspectives and experiences. This promotes compassion and strengthens relationships.

- **Respect and Appreciation:** Show respect for others' boundaries, opinions, and individuality. Express appreciation for their contributions and acknowledge their strengths.

- **Open and Non-Defensive Communication:** Create an environment where both parties feel safe expressing themselves without fear of judgment or criticism. Avoid becoming defensive and instead listen with an open mind and a willingness to understand.

Mind Over Mood

Chapter 8

Stress Management

Stress has inevitably become a part of our lives in today's fast-paced and demanding environment. Whether it's work-related pressures, relationship challenges, financial burdens, or personal expectations, stress can have a significant impact on our emotional well-being. By understanding stress and implementing effective strategies, you can enhance your emotional resilience and overall well-being.

Understanding Stress and Its Impact

Stress is the body's natural response to any perceived threat or demand, whether physical, emotional, or psychological. It triggers a cascade of physiological and psychological reactions, preparing us to face the challenge or danger at hand. However, prolonged or excessive stress can have detrimental effects on our mental and physical health.

Stress Reduction Techniques

To effectively manage stress, it is essential to adopt techniques that promote relaxation, reduce tension, and restore emotional balance. This section presents a range of proven stress reduction techniques that individuals can incorporate into their daily lives. Some of these techniques include:

- **Deep Breathing:** Deep breathing exercises help activate the body's relaxation response, slowing down the heart rate and calming the mind. Techniques like diaphragmatic breathing, box breathing, or progressive muscle relaxation can be effective in reducing stress levels.

- **Mindfulness and Meditation:** Mindfulness practices involve intentionally focusing one's attention on the present moment without judgment. Meditation techniques, such as mindfulness meditation, loving-kindness meditation, or body scan meditation, can help cultivate a sense of inner peace and decrease stress.

- Physical Exercise: Engaging in regular physical activity, whether it's jogging, yoga, swimming, or dancing, can have significant stress-reducing effects. Exercise releases endorphins, which are natural mood enhancers, and helps relieve muscular tension, providing a healthy outlet for stress.

- Time Management: Learning effective time management skills can help individuals prioritize tasks, set realistic goals, and create a sense of control over their responsibilities. By organizing their time efficiently, individuals can reduce stress associated with feeling overwhelmed or rushed.

Creating a Balanced Lifestyle

A well-rounded and balanced lifestyle plays a crucial role in managing stress effectively. This section explores the importance of self-care practices and healthy habits that contribute to emotional well-being. Some key aspects covered in this section include:

- **Sleep and Rest:** Adequate sleep is essential for stress management and overall well-being. The chapter emphasizes the importance of establishing a regular sleep routine, creating a conducive sleep environment, and implementing relaxation techniques to promote quality rest.

- **Nutrition:** A balanced and nutritious diet plays a significant role in supporting our physical and mental health. This section provides guidance on adopting healthy eating habits, including consuming a variety of nutrient-rich foods, staying hydrated, and minimizing the intake of stress-inducing substances like caffeine and alcohol.

- **Leisure and Recreation:** Engaging in enjoyable activities and hobbies is vital for stress reduction and enhancing overall life satisfaction. This section explores the benefits of recreational pursuits, such as spending time in nature, pursuing creative outlets, or participating in sports or social activities.

Mind Over Mood

- **Social Support:** Building and nurturing a strong support network is essential for stress management. It highlights the significance of maintaining healthy relationships, seeking support from loved ones or support groups, and cultivating a sense of belonging and connection.

Self-Care Practices for Emotional Well-being

Self-care is a fundamental aspect of managing stress and fostering emotional well-being. This section explores various self-care practices that individuals can incorporate into their daily lives. It emphasizes the importance of self-compassion, setting boundaries, and prioritizing activities that promote relaxation and rejuvenation. Some self-care practices covered in this section include:

- **Journaling and Expressive Writing:** Writing down thoughts, emotions, and experiences can provide a therapeutic outlet for stress and help gain clarity. This section guides individuals on how to

Mind Over Mood

incorporate journaling and expressive writing techniques into their self-care routine.

- **Mindful Activities:** Engaging in activities that promote mindfulness, such as practicing yoga, taking mindful walks, or enjoying a hot bath, can help individuals reconnect with the present moment and alleviate stress.

- **Relaxation Techniques:** This section introduces various relaxation techniques, including progressive muscle relaxation, guided imagery, aromatherapy, or listening to calming music. These techniques aim to induce relaxation responses in the body and mind.

- **Digital Detox:** In today's digital age, it is essential to set boundaries with technology to reduce stress levels. This section provides tips on implementing a digital detox, such as limiting screen time, establishing tech-free zones, and practicing mindful technology use.

Part III:
Integrating
Acceptance and
Mastery

Chapter 9

Embracing Emotional Authenticity

Honoring Your True Feelings

Authenticity is a powerful concept when it comes to emotions. Honoring your true feelings means acknowledging and accepting them without judgment or suppression. It involves being honest with yourself about what you genuinely feel and allowing those emotions to exist without resistance.

In today's society, there is often pressure to conform to certain emotional norms or to mask our true feelings in order to fit in or avoid discomfort. However, by denying or suppressing our emotions, we hinder our ability to understand ourselves fully and prevent genuine connections with others.

Honoring your true feelings requires self-awareness and the willingness to be vulnerable. It means being

Mind Over Mood

in touch with your emotions, even if they are uncomfortable or difficult to face. Whether it's joy, sadness, anger, or fear, each emotion carries valuable information about your experiences and needs.

By honoring your true feelings, you develop a deeper understanding of yourself. This understanding allows you to make more informed decisions, set boundaries, and communicate effectively with others. When you honor your true feelings, you give yourself permission to be authentic and live in alignment with your values.

Being Genuine and Authentic

Being genuine and authentic means expressing yourself honestly and transparently. It involves aligning your actions, thoughts, and emotions with your true self, rather than conforming to societal expectations or seeking approval from others.

In a world that often values appearances and masks, embracing emotional authenticity can be a transformative experience. It allows you to break free from the pressure to please others and fosters a sense of self-acceptance and self-respect. When you show up as your authentic self, you attract genuine connections and build relationships based on trust and mutual understanding.

Emotional authenticity also requires courage. It may involve taking risks, speaking your truth, and confronting potential conflicts or disagreements. However, the rewards of being genuine far outweigh the temporary discomfort that may arise. When you live authentically, you create space for growth, personal fulfillment, and deep connections.

Living in Alignment with Your Values

Living in alignment with your values is an essential aspect of embracing emotional authenticity. Values serve as guiding principles that shape your beliefs, behaviors, and choices. When your emotions and actions align with your values, you experience a sense of congruence and fulfillment.

To live in alignment with your values, it's crucial to identify and clarify what truly matters to you.

Channel your energy to what gives meaning and purpose to your life. Consider the qualities and virtues you admire in others and aspire to cultivate within yourself. These values may include integrity, compassion, honesty, growth, or connection, among others.

Once you have identified your values, make a conscious effort to align your emotions and actions with them. Ask yourself if your choices and behaviors reflect the principles you hold dear. By making decisions that are consistent with your values, you cultivate a sense of authenticity and integrity.

Living in alignment with your values also means setting boundaries and saying no when necessary. It involves prioritizing self-care, respecting your limits, and ensuring that your emotional well-being remains a top priority. When you honor your values and live authentically, you create a life that is true to yourself and fosters genuine happiness and fulfillment.

Embracing emotional authenticity is a journey of self-discovery and growth. It requires self-reflection, self-compassion, and a willingness to embrace vulnerability. As you honor your true feelings, be genuine and authentic, and live in alignment with your values, you will cultivate a deep sense of self-acceptance and create a more meaningful and fulfilling life.

Chapter 10

Sustaining Emotional Growth

Creating Supportive Environments

Here, we delve into the importance of creating supportive environments to sustain emotional growth. While personal growth and emotional mastery begin from within, the external environment plays a significant role in nurturing and reinforcing these positive changes. By consciously surrounding ourselves with supportive people, places, and circumstances, we can enhance our emotional well-being and maintain our progress.

One key aspect of creating a supportive environment is building a network of individuals who uplift and inspire us. Surrounding ourselves with positive and like-minded people can have a profound impact on our emotional growth. These individuals can provide encouragement, understanding, and constructive feedback when needed. They can serve as role models and mentors, sharing their own experiences and wisdom to guide us on our journey. Building authentic and meaningful connections with others fosters a sense of belonging and creates a safe space for emotional expression and growth.

Additionally, the physical spaces we inhabit can greatly influence our emotional well-being. Creating an environment that promotes calmness, creativity, and positivity can contribute to our emotional growth. This could involve decluttering and organizing our living or workspace, incorporating elements of nature, and personalizing our surroundings with items that hold meaning and evoke positive emotions. Such environments can provide a sense of tranquility and serve as a sanctuary where we can retreat and recharge.

Furthermore, the circumstances and activities we engage in can either hinder or support our emotional growth. It is important to assess the various aspects of our lives, such as our career, hobbies, and daily routines, to ensure they align with our values and contribute to our overall well-being. This may involve making intentional choices and adjustments to create a lifestyle that nurtures our emotional growth. For example, if a particular job or relationship consistently drains our energy and stifles our emotional growth, it may be necessary to reevaluate and make changes to create a more supportive and fulfilling environment.

Continual Self-Reflection and Learning

Continual self-reflection and learning are crucial elements of sustaining emotional growth. By regularly examining our thoughts, feelings, and behaviors, we gain valuable insights into ourselves and the factors that influence our emotional well-being. This introspective process allows us to identify patterns, triggers, and areas for improvement, enabling us to make conscious choices that align with our emotional goals.

Self-reflection involves setting aside dedicated time for introspection and contemplation. This can be achieved through practices such as journaling, meditation, or engaging in mindful activities like walking in nature or engaging in creative pursuits. During these moments of reflection, we can explore our emotions, thoughts, and experiences, allowing us to gain a deeper understanding of ourselves and our emotional landscape. Self-reflection also helps us to cultivate self-awareness and develop a more compassionate and accepting attitude toward ourselves and others.

In addition to self-reflection, ongoing learning is essential for sustaining emotional growth. This involves seeking out resources, knowledge, and experiences that expand our understanding of emotions, personal development, and effective strategies for emotional mastery.

We can engage in various learning opportunities such as reading books, attending workshops or seminars, participating in therapy or coaching, and seeking out the guidance of experts in the field of emotional well-being.

By embracing a growth mindset and actively pursuing personal development, we create an environment of continuous learning. This allows us to discover new insights, perspectives, and tools that can support our emotional growth journey. Learning from others, whether through their experiences, teachings, or research, can provide us with valuable strategies and perspectives that enhance our emotional intelligence and empower us to navigate life's challenges with greater resilience and effectiveness.

Nurturing Emotional Growth in Relationships

Our relationships have a profound impact on our emotional well-being and growth. In Chapter 10, we explore the importance of nurturing emotional growth within our relationships and the role they play in supporting our journey toward emotional mastery.

Healthy and fulfilling relationships are characterized by open communication, trust, empathy, and mutual support. They provide a nurturing space where we can express our emotions authentically and feel understood and validated. When our emotions are acknowledged and accepted by those close to us, it cultivates a sense of emotional safety and encourages us to explore and navigate our emotional landscape with greater confidence.

Nurturing emotional growth in relationships involves cultivating effective communication skills. This includes active listening, empathy, and assertive expression of our emotions and needs. When we listen attentively to others, seek to understand their perspective, and respond with empathy, we foster deeper connections and create an environment that encourages emotional growth for all parties involved.

Mind Over Mood

Likewise, expressing our own emotions and needs assertively, while also respecting the emotions and needs of others, allows for healthy and constructive emotional exchanges.

In addition to communication, nurturing emotional growth in relationships requires fostering emotional intimacy.

This involves creating an atmosphere of trust, vulnerability, and authenticity, where both parties feel comfortable expressing their true selves and their emotions without fear of judgment or rejection. Emotional intimacy deepens connections and strengthens the bond between individuals, providing a foundation for mutual support and growth.

Furthermore, it is essential to establish and maintain healthy boundaries within relationships to support emotional growth. Boundaries ensure that our emotional well-being is protected and respected, allowing us to maintain our individuality while also engaging in healthy and fulfilling connections with

Mind Over Mood

others. By communicating our boundaries effectively and respecting the boundaries of others, we create a space where emotional growth can flourish.

Conclusion

"Mind Over Mood" is a transformative journey that empowers individuals to embrace their emotional landscape with authenticity, compassion, and self-awareness. Throughout this book, we have explored the profound impact our emotions have on our well-being, relationships, and overall life satisfaction.

By delving into the depths of our feelings, we have learned that acknowledging and accepting them is the first step towards emotional mastery. It is through this process that we begin to understand the valuable messages our emotions hold and how they can guide us towards personal growth and fulfillment.

The book has provided practical tools and techniques to cultivate emotional intelligence, such as mindfulness, self-reflection, and effective communication. We have discovered the power of self-compassion, allowing ourselves to experience a

Mind Over Mood

full range of emotions without judgment, and embracing vulnerability as a pathway to genuine connection.

Moreover, "Mind Over Mood" has emphasized the importance of developing resilience in the face of adversity. It has taught us to navigate through challenging emotions, transforming them into opportunities for self-discovery, resilience, and growth. We have witnessed the immense strength that lies within us when we learn to harness our emotions rather than be controlled by them.

Ultimately, this book has encouraged us to become the masters of our emotions, to navigate the ebb and flow of our internal world with grace and wisdom. It has shown us that emotional intelligence is not just an innate trait but a skill that can be learned and nurtured over time.

As we close this chapter, let us embark on a new journey—one that embraces our authentic selves, cultivates empathy for others, and allows us to forge deeper connections with those around us.

Mind Over Mood

May we remember that our emotions are not to be feared or suppressed but rather embraced and understood, leading us towards a more meaningful and fulfilling life.

In the words of Carl Jung, "I am not what happened to me, I am what I choose to become." Let us choose to become emotionally resilient individuals who accept, understand, and master our emotions, fostering a world of empathy, compassion, and personal growth.

Mind Over Mood

BONUS

Resources and Exercises

Recommended Books and Articles

1. *"FIND YOUR CALM: Unleash your full potential" by John L. Fisher*

This groundbreaking book explores the Key guides to Controlling your Feelings, Mastering your Emotions and Becoming better.

2. *"Emotional Intelligence: Why It Can Matter More Than IQ" by Daniel Goleman*

- This groundbreaking book explores the concept of emotional intelligence and its impact on personal and professional success. Goleman presents scientific research and practical strategies for understanding and managing emotions effectively.

3. *"Daring Greatly: How the Courage to Be Vulnerable Transforms the Way We Live, Love, Parent, and Lead" by Brené Brown*

Mind Over Mood

- Brown explores the power of vulnerability and encourages readers to embrace their feelings and open up to authentic experiences.

The book offers valuable insights into emotional acceptance, self-compassion, and wholehearted living.

4. "The Upside of Stress: Why Stress Is Good for You, and How to Get Good at It" by Kelly McGonigal

- McGonigal challenges the common perception of stress and highlights its potential benefits. She provides practical strategies for harnessing stress to improve emotional resilience and achieve personal growth.

Article Recommendations:

1. "The Power of Emotional Acceptance" by Susan David (Harvard Business Review)

- In this article, Susan David discusses the importance of accepting our emotions rather than suppressing or ignoring them. She provides practical strategies for emotional acceptance, highlighting the positive impact it can have on personal and professional well-being.

2. *"Mastering Your Emotions: Tips for Emotional Regulation" by Psych Central*

- This article offers practical tips and techniques for mastering emotions and enhancing emotional regulation. It covers topics such as identifying and labeling emotions, managing stress, and developing healthy coping mechanisms.

3. *"Why You Shouldn't Fear Negative Emotions" by Adam Grant (The New York Times)*

- Adam Grant explores the value of negative emotions and how they can be harnessed for personal growth and resilience. The article challenges the notion that only positive emotions are desirable and provides a fresh perspective on emotional acceptance.

4. *"The Science of Emotional Intelligence" by John D. Mayer and Peter Salovey (Psychology Today)*

- This article delves into the science behind emotional intelligence, explaining its various components and their implications for personal and social well-being. It offers practical insights and exercises for developing emotional intelligence skills.

5. *"Emotional Agility: The Key to Resilience" by Susan David (TED Talk)*

- This TED Talk by Susan David explores the concept of emotional agility and its role in building resilience. She shares strategies for navigating difficult emotions and adapting to change, empowering individuals to thrive in challenging circumstances.

Guided Meditation and Visualization Exercises

Exercise 1: Embracing Emotional Awareness

Take a seat peacefully in a place where you won't be disturbed. Take a few deep breaths and close your eyes to let yourself unwind and let go of any tension.. As you settle into a state of calm, bring your attention to your emotions.

Visualize a beautiful garden in your mind's eye. Picture yourself standing at the entrance, ready to explore. This garden represents your emotional landscape, filled with various emotions, each like a different flower.

Now, imagine walking through the garden and noticing the different flowers representing your emotions. Take your time to observe each one without judgment or attachment. Notice their colors, shapes, and scents. As you come across each emotion, allow yourself to acknowledge its presence and accept it as a natural part of your being.

If you encounter any challenging emotions, remind yourself that they, too, have a purpose and deserve acknowledgment. Approach them with curiosity and compassion. Spend a few moments with each emotion, accepting its presence and allowing it to be.

As you continue to explore the garden, notice how each emotion is interconnected, just like the flowers in a vibrant ecosystem. Embrace the ebb and flow of emotions, recognizing that they are transient and ever-changing.

When you're ready, slowly open your eyes, bringing your awareness back to the present moment.

Take a deep breath, carrying the acceptance and awareness you cultivated in the garden into your daily life.

Exercise 2: Anchoring Inner Stability

Find a comfortable position either seated or lying down, ensuring that your body feels relaxed and supported. Gently close your eyes and begin by taking a few deep, slow breaths, allowing your body and mind to relax.

Visualize yourself standing on the shore of a calm, serene lake. Feel the warmth of the sun on your skin and the gentle breeze against your face. As you look out at the lake, notice its stillness and clarity, reflecting the peace within you.

Now, imagine a sturdy and grounded tree nearby, with deep roots that extend into the earth. Visualize yourself becoming one with the tree, feeling your own roots growing from the soles of your feet, reaching down into the ground. Feel the stability and strength that comes from this connection.

With each breath, imagine drawing up nourishing energy from the earth through your roots, up into your body, filling you with a sense of stability and grounding. As you exhale, release any tension or unease, allowing it to be absorbed by the earth.

Observe them without bias or attachment, letting them flow through you. Allow them to flow through you, observing them without judgment or attachment. Remember that you are like the tree, capable of remaining steady and resilient even in the face of challenging emotions.

Stay in this state of groundedness for as long as you wish, knowing that you can return to this visualization whenever you need to find inner stability. When you're ready to conclude the exercise, slowly bring your awareness back to your physical surroundings, taking a few moments to savor the tranquility you've cultivated.

Note: It's important to consult a professional if you're dealing with deep emotional struggles or mental health issues.

These exercises are intended as general tools for self-reflection and relaxation and are not a substitute for professional help.

Journal Prompts for Emotional Exploration

1. Reflect on a recent situation where you felt a strong emotional response. What were the underlying emotions driving your reaction? How did you handle or cope with those emotions at the time?

2. Describe a time when you found it challenging to accept and acknowledge your feelings. What were the consequences of avoiding or suppressing those emotions? How could you have approached the situation differently?

3. Write about a specific emotion that you tend to resist or struggle with. What might be the root cause of this resistance? How could understanding and accepting this emotion enhance your emotional well-being?

4. Explore a childhood experience that significantly influenced your emotional development. How do you think this experience shaped your current relationship with emotions? Are there any unresolved emotions from that time that you need to address?

5. Consider a recent situation where you acted impulsively based on an intense emotion. What could you have done differently to respond more mindfully and effectively?

How can you cultivate emotional intelligence in similar situations in the future?

6. Reflect on a past failure or disappointment that evoked strong negative emotions. How did you initially respond to these emotions? Looking back, how could you have utilized those emotions as a catalyst for personal growth or positive change?

7. Write about a recurring pattern in your emotional responses that you would like to understand better. What triggers this pattern? Are there any deeper emotions or beliefs connected to it?

How might shifting your perspective or mindset help you master this emotional pattern?

8. Explore the relationship between vulnerability and emotional acceptance. How does embracing vulnerability contribute to a healthier emotional life? Describe a situation where you allowed yourself to be vulnerable and experienced growth as a result.

9. Reflect on a time when you received criticism or negative feedback. How did you initially react

emotionally, and how did that affect your ability to learn from the feedback? How can you approach criticism more constructively in the future?

10. Consider a relationship in your life where you find it challenging to express or communicate your emotions effectively. What fears or barriers might be preventing you from opening up? How could you work towards creating a more emotionally open and supportive dynamic in that relationship?

Remember, the process of exploring and accepting your emotions is personal and unique to each individual. Take your time with these prompts, allow yourself to dive deep, and be gentle with yourself throughout the journey.

Emotional Support Resources

Emotional well-being is a vital aspect of our lives, and understanding how to accept and manage our feelings is crucial for personal growth and overall happiness. If you're seeking additional emotional

Mind Over Mood

support and resources to complement your journey of Mind Over Mood, here are some suggestions:

1. Therapy and Counseling:

- Individual Therapy: Engage in one-on-one sessions with a licensed therapist who specializes in emotions and emotional regulation.

- Group Therapy: Join a support group where you can share experiences, learn from others, and gain valuable insights into managing emotions.

- Online Counseling: Explore digital platforms that offer convenient and accessible therapy sessions via video calls or chat.

2. Books and Workbooks:

- "The Language of Emotions" by Karla McLaren: Discover how emotions can guide and transform your life in this insightful book.

- "Emotional Intelligence" by Daniel Goleman: Gain a deeper understanding of emotional intelligence and learn strategies to enhance your emotional well-being.

3. Meditation and Mindfulness:

Mind Over Mood

- Headspace: Access the popular meditation app that provides guided meditations, mindfulness exercises, and tools to promote emotional balance.

- Insight Timer: Discover a vast library of free guided meditations, music tracks, and talks from various teachers to support your emotional well-being.

- Calm: Experience relaxing sounds, guided meditations, and sleep stories designed to reduce stress and cultivate emotional resilience.

4. Online Communities and Forums:

- r/EmotionalIntelligence (Reddit): Engage with a supportive online community dedicated to discussing emotional intelligence, sharing experiences, and seeking advice.

- Psych Central Forums: Join these forums to connect with others, seek support, and participate in discussions on various emotional well-being topics.

5. Emotional Support Apps: - Sanvello: This app offers resources, mood tracking, coping tools, and access to peer support groups.

Mind Over Mood

- Youper: Utilize artificial intelligence to track your mood, journal your emotions, and access guided conversations to understand and manage your feelings.

Remember, seeking support is a courageous step towards personal growth. Utilize these resources to foster self-awareness, emotional acceptance, and develop strategies for mastering your emotions.

Mind Over Mood